LIVING THE
EXTRAORDINARY
LIFE

© 2005 by Charles F. Stanley

Published in Nashville, Tennessee, by Thomas Nelson. Thomas Nelson is a registered trademark of Thomas Nelson, Inc.

Thomas Nelson, Inc., titles may be purchased in bulk for educational, business, fund-raising, or sales promotional use. For information, please e-mail SpecialMarkets@ThomasNelson.com.

Unless otherwise noted, Scripture quotations are from the NEW AMERICAN STANDARD BIBLE®. © 1960, 1962, 1963, 1968, 1971, 1972, 1973, 1975, 1977, 1995 by The Lockman Foundation. Used by permission. www.Lockman.org.

Scripture quotations noted NKJV are from THE NEW KING JAMES VERSION®. © 1979, 1980, 1982 Thomas Nelson, Inc., Publishers.

Scripture quotations noted NIV are from the HOLY BIBLE: NEW INTERNATIONAL VERSION®. © 1973, 1978, 1984 by International Bible Society. Used by permission of Zondervan Publishing House. All rights reserved.

Scripture quotations noted NLT are from *The Living Bible,* © 1971. Used by permission of Tyndale House Publishers, Inc., Wheaton, Illinois 60189. All rights reserved.

Scripture quotations noted KJV are from the KING JAMES VERSION.

Scripture quotations noted NLV are from the NEW LIFE VERSION.

Library of Congress Cataloging-in-Publication Data

Stanley, Charles F.
    Living the extraordinary life : 9 principles to discover it / Charles F. Stanley.
      p. cm.
    Includes bibliographical references
    ISBN 978-0-7852-6611-2 (hardcover)
    ISBN 978-1-4002-8008-7 (trade paper)
    1. Spiritual life—Christianity. 2. Christian life. I. Title.
BV4501.3.S734 2005
248.4—dc22

                                    2005012266

Printed in the United States of America

08 09 10 11 12 RRD 6 5 4 3 2 1

LIVING THE
EXTRAORDINARY
LIFE

*Nine Principles
to Discover It*

CHARLES F. STANLEY

THOMAS NELSON
Since 1798

NASHVILLE   DALLAS   MEXICO CITY   RIO DE JANEIRO   BEIJING

It is with great joy that I dedicate this book to my dear friend and colleague Robert (Bob) Schipper, whose faithful service both to me and In Touch Ministries has truly been extraordinary.

CONTENTS

Contents

PREFACE

Life in the twenty-first century is tough. The world is becoming increasingly volatile. Despite unprecedented technological, scientific, and educational advances, our society grows more fragile with each passing year. Institutional, cultural, and moral foundations upon which we have come to depend are rapidly decaying, and pressures inside and outside the home sometimes overwhelm us.

Are you wrestling against forces that seem out of your control? Is life's treadmill going faster than you are? If you answer yes, like most people today, you are running your own life, moving from crisis to crisis without slowing down. Like a sick person who ignores the dull pain in his spine, you work harder and spend more money trying to distract yourself from a reality that might interrupt your life. If the pain becomes intolerable, you'll seek help. And you may learn that your condition is worse than you thought—that it might have been prevented had you dealt with it earlier.

During the past seven decades, I have sometimes run myself weary on that same treadmill. I have strived, failed, achieved, stumbled, and been lifted up. I have listened to the advice of my peers and heeded the wisdom of God. I've seen the top of the "spiritual mountain" and been caught in a valley so deep I thought I would never find my way out. Throughout my life's journey, I have come to understand one thing clearly: only God can help you to live a truly extraordinary life.

There is a bedrock of truth upon which we can stand—a truth so strong no tide can move it. Because we are followers of Christ, our confidence in unstable times lies in an unchanging God who provides steady anchors of faith and assurance. When I think of how near God is and yet how often we fail to see Him, I am reminded of a photography excursion I once took to Switzerland in hopes of photographing a legendary mountain: the Matterhorn. After a four-hour train ride to the town of Zermatt, I was greeted by a storm of rain, sleet, and snow that persisted for three days. I surveyed the entire area, but never even saw the foot of the mountain, let alone anything worth photographing. On my last night there, I shared my disappointment with the Lord. I had come a long way for the sole purpose of taking a picture of that mountain, and I knew He understood.

Before I lay down to sleep, I opened the shutters of my window to let in the fresh air. I woke at 5:20 AM and looked out at the morning. Even today I can still see it—the Matterhorn, all 14,691 feet of her glorious whiteness, hovered above me like a giant cobra. The sky in the background was completely black, and a halo of light illuminated the entire mountain. It was as if God said, "See what happens when you wait for Me."

Later that day, I rode the cable car to nearly 12,000 feet, but the best shots I got were the ones I took from my hotel window. The building in front of me was just low enough that I could shoot over it, and I had an absolutely perfect view. To this day, my picture of the Matterhorn is one of my favorites. The awesome lesson I learned from this experience was that God is always near—whether we can see Him or not. I'd been there for three days searching in vain through a blanket of fog. Yet all that time, the peak was right there in front of me.

God's promises are like that. If you will slow down and focus your attention enough to see them, you can appropriate them for your life in unimaginable ways. In the midst of spiraling instability, it is easy to forget your true source of strength. Yet even as you stumble along life's wearying path, He walks with you—through disillusionment, discouragement, and doubt. He is never turned away by your wayward acts. He knows that on your own, you can do nothing, but that through Christ, you can and will succeed. He who began a good work in you will perfect it until the day of Christ Jesus (PHIL. 1:6).

When you place your hope in temporal things—money, social status, achievements, acceptance, or even the love of your family and friends—your foundation will inevitably crumble. Worldly comforts are no defense against the tumultuous storms that life often delivers. Your identity must be based on something greater than what the world offers if you are to stand strong.

As the old saying goes, life is not about *who* you are; it's about *whose* you are. And whose you are has essentially nothing to do with you and everything to do with Him. Your challenge is to get out of the way so God can move in and through you. He has a distinct purpose for each of His children, and He wants you to understand that purpose. When you finally see how beloved you are and how great is your calling, you will begin to live for God through His power.

The Bible offers us numerous principles for walking successfully with God, for living the extraordinary life. I do not have the space to detail each and every one of them here—you can find a more extensive treatment in the *Life Principles Bible*. In this book, I will address nine time-tested truths that God reveals to us through Scripture and discuss how we as believers can live extraordinary lives.

What is the extraordinary life? It is the life sustained by an inner peace and joy in the good times as well as the bad. I can honestly say, after all these years, that I am finally at a place where I know how to face anxiety, fear, and the pressures that accompany life this side of heaven. My ultimate goal now is to live in undisturbed union with Jesus Christ, and by His strength, I am closer than ever.

Becoming the masterpiece God created you to be is a lifelong process in which He is continually shaping you into a unique reflection of His Son. It is my prayer that you will embrace each one of these principles fully and, in doing so, discover the extraordinary life God has planned for you.

At the end of each chapter, you will find a suggested Bible reading, a prayer, and a place to record your thoughts regarding the principle. I also encourage you to visit the In Touch ministries web site at www.InTouch.org, where you will find a more in-depth study of the principles in this book, as well as numerous courses on the foundations of our faith. When you log on to our Web site, take advantage of the opportunity provided to share with me your personal journey and to connect with other Christians around the world.

INTRODUCTION

YOUR LIFE AS A MASTERPIECE

On April 12, 1945, President Franklin Delano Roosevelt was at the Little White House in Warm Springs, Georgia, sitting for a portrait, when he died suddenly of a cerebral hemorrhage. The *Unfinished Portrait,* as it is called, remains on its easel looking out on the world much as it did when artist Elizabeth Shoumatoff lay her brush down at the sight of the president's collapse. The watercolor likeness of the president shows a man of inner strength and resolve. However, photographs taken days before and placed alongside the artist's canvas for reference reveal a much different man, a national leader who was emotionally and physically taxed from the political load he bore.

Later, Madame Shoumatoff returned to her work on the president's portrait. Nevertheless, she did not choose to finish the watercolor she had originally begun. It was complete in its own right. Instead, she painted a new picture, a handsome rendering of President Roosevelt that portrayed his confidence and charisma. We see no visible flaws in this likeness; rather, we see a man of integrity, courage, and conviction who profoundly affected the world in which he lived.

Do you ever wonder what a portrait of you would reveal? If an honest and capable painter depicted you, what would the world see? Integrity, courage, and conviction? Or dishonesty, fear, and doubt? Most people live behind a façade of sorts—somewhat like the second picture of President Roosevelt—which reveals only a part of who they are. Afraid of rejection, they hide their flaws from the world and even from themselves.

Thankfully there is one person—the One who matters most—who sees all of our flaws and failures but loves us completely the way we are. Just as Madame Shoumatoff chose to focus her attention on the inner beauty of the subject she painted, God sees in each of His children the redemption and promise won by His Son at Calvary. You are His masterpiece, a work conceived in grace and love. And if you allow Him to, He will paint the colors of your life in a way that glorifies Him: "We are His workmanship, created in Christ Jesus for good works, which God prepared beforehand that we should walk in them" (EPH. 2:10 NKJV).

By God's loving grace, each of us was created in the image of Christ. Though our lives, from a human perspective, are still on the canvas, God has seen the final portraits. He has eternal eyes, and He knows exactly what part of our lives need His greatest attention. Every frustration, every disappointment, and every joy has a purpose. He causes all things to work together for good for those who love Him and are called according to His purpose (ROM. 8:28).

For many people, this is a hard concept to grasp. You may see your life as incomplete, much like the unfinished portrait of President Roosevelt. But God views you from a totally different perspective. When He sees your life, He sees a person of worth and great promise.

THE TRUTH OF WHO YOU ARE IN CHRIST WILL SET YOU FREE

Back in the fifties, I used to watch a television program called *The Life of Riley*. (Some readers are old enough to remember watching it.) The idea was to portray a life that everyone would want to experience. During the opening credits, the star of the series was shown lying back in a hammock with his arms folded behind his head, while others hurriedly cut grass and cleaned the yard behind him. However, as the story unfolded, viewers quickly saw how unpredictable and funny life could be. Somehow, Riley always came out on top, unscathed by the episode and back in his hammock.

But Riley was only a television character created by a group of talented writers, actors, and directors. Tragically, many people spend their entire lives trying to live the life of Riley. They turn to money and friends for the fulfillment that only God can offer, and they are disillusioned when they feel empty inside.

Fulfillment in a material sense does not guarantee that the inner hunger residing deep within our souls will be satisfied. True fulfillment does not come as a result of owning a large home, driving a new car, or having money in the bank. True fulfillment is the result of having a personal relationship with Jesus Christ.

Some of the richest people in the world are the loneliest. They use their money to travel and buy all that their hearts desire, but their search for true happiness continues. Many of them mistakenly believe that genuine fulfillment is one financial merger away. What they really need is a heart and soul merger.

Solomon wrote,

I enlarged my works: I built houses for myself, I planted vineyards for myself; I made gardens and parks for myself and I planted in them all kinds of fruit trees . . . I collected for myself silver and gold and the treasure of kings and provinces . . . Then I became great and increased more than all who preceded me in Jerusalem . . . All that my eyes desired I did not refuse them. I did not withhold my heart from any pleasure, for my heart was pleased because of all my labor and this was my reward. . . . Thus I considered all my activities which my hands had done and the labor which I had exerted, and behold all was vanity and striving after wind and there was no profit under the sun. (ECCL. 2:4–11)

Life at its best is not without trouble and pain; rather, it encompasses the fullness of experiences that lead to a deeper wisdom and knowledge of God's grace. Through the trials of life, our heavenly Father teaches us, directs us, and shapes us into truly glorious people. Solomon wrote,

> Trust in the LORD with all your heart
> And do not lean on your own understanding.
> In all your ways acknowledge Him,
> And He will make your paths straight.
> Do not be wise in your own eyes;
> Fear the LORD and turn away from evil. (PROV. 3:5–7)

When we place our trust in Christ, we essentially abandon ourselves to Him and willingly let go of the things that captivate our fleshly attention. We agree with God to resist the temptation to get caught up in the fray of our society.

Material possessions, financial security, and relationships cannot fill the deep, unsettling voids that accompany life. Jesus realized that the powerful hunger in our hearts yields easily to selfish desires. That was why He told His disciples to "seek first His kingdom and His righteousness; and all these things will be added to you" (MATT. 6:33).

Everything you will ever need is already yours in Jesus Christ. Giving yourself to Him does not mean you will come out with less. It means you will come out with the best. When we give ourselves to God, He always gives much more in return. However, His dividends may not include owning a house at the beach, a mountain cottage, and a home in the city. Some of the happiest people I have known are those who have less, yet are spiritually wealthy and emotionally stable, all because they have learned to place their trust in something that can never be taken from them—a loving relationship with the Lord Jesus Christ (LUKE 10:42).

You may be a Christian who attends church faithfully, prays daily, and even gives generously. Yet if you place your confidence in your own intellect and power instead of trusting God, you are standing in the way of His highest blessing for your life. Regardless of how we appear to others, God sees every aspect of us. He knows what each original portrait looks like.

He sees your life from beginning to end, and because He loves you, He works all things in and through your life for His glory. Many times what seems painful to you on the outside is really God working on the inside to bring you to the end of yourself and ultimately closer to Him. His primary goal is not to make you great, but to love you greatly, to experience intimate fellowship with you, and to prepare you for eternity.

You are His masterpiece, and He has given His Word as a testimony to the love and joy He has for you. ZEPHANIAH 3:17 declares, "The LORD your God is in your midst, a victorious warrior. He will exult over you with joy, He will be quiet in His love, He will rejoice over you with shouts of joy."

God rejoices over you, though He knows your life is still in the process of becoming all that He has planned—though you are not yet what you will be when you step into His eternal presence. Until that time, He is shaping your life, conforming you to the image of His Son.

Amid the uncertainty and pressures surrounding you, Jesus is at your side to strengthen and encourage you. When your eyes are fixed on Him and not the world around you, you begin to see life differently. Instead of your striving to live up to others' standards, the Holy Spirit will teach you to dwell on the things of God, which are pure and honoring to Jesus Christ.

This does not mean that you will avoid the feelings of rejection or loneliness. Jesus felt both, and yet the goal of accomplishing the Father's will was always before Him. He knew that in order to complete His mission, He would have to endure the trials of life. For Jesus, this meant the Cross and physical death.

You can walk in victory because Jesus is your example, and His Spirit lives in you. How could He possibly bear the weight of all our sins and still remain victorious? God had given Him an eternal perspective; He knew the Resurrection was a completed fact. And after three days He rose to walk in victory. God gives you strength and power too through the presence of the Holy Spirit (ROM. 8:11).

God uses every frustration, fear, and feeling of hopelessness like colors on an artist's palette to move your life toward completion. Hardship, however difficult, reminds us of our need for the Father and chases us to Him, where we belong. One day you will see the wonder and splendor of God's work and understand the purpose behind each of your trials. Like an artist blending both dark and light colors to achieve a beautiful portrait, He will work in your life to create a masterpiece.

In Deuteronomy, God gives us a spiritual principle to use as a compass for our lives: our identity must be based in Christ. Is your heart pointed toward God? Or is it focused on selfish desires? "You shall do what is right and good in the sight of the LORD, that it may be well with you and that you may go in and possess the good land which the LORD swore to give your fathers" (6:18).

"He will love you and bless you and multiply you," wrote Moses (DEUT. 7:13). This is the result of obedience. Though this principle was given to Israel, it also is a command for us to heed. When you declare your love for the Lord and submit your life to Him, He will bless you, guide you, and bring a sense of sincere fulfillment to your heart.

SUGGESTED BIBLE READING

Ephesians 2:10; Romans 8:11–28; Isaiah 29:16;
Ecclesiastes 2:4–11; Proverbs 3:5–7; Matthew
6:33; and Luke 10:42.

PRAYER

Dear heavenly Father, I want to become the
masterpiece You desire me to be. I pray that You would
help me to put away my self-reliance and striving for
worldly affirmation and look to You as the source of
my worth. Please create in me a new heart and a true
understanding of my position in Christ Jesus. Amen.

JOURNAL QUESTIONS

- For what purpose did God create you?

_____

_____

_____

_____

_____

- What is the true source of your identity? What should be
  the true source of your identity?

_____

_____

_____

_____

_____

- What steps will you take today to know Christ more?

_____

_____

_____

_____

_____

Find out more about God's plan for reshaping
your life and priorities at
www.InTouch.org today.

PRINCIPLE
1

COMPLETE SURRENDER TO GOD
BRINGS COMPLETE LIFE

I recently heard a story that makes a profound point about surrender. Some time ago a radio station reported news of a stolen VW Bug in California. The police staged an intense search for the vehicle and the man who stole it, even to the point of making announcements on local radio stations to contact him. On the front seat of the stolen car sat a box of crackers that, unbeknownst to the thief, was laced with poison. The car's owner had intended to use the crackers as rat bait. You see, the police and the owner of the car were more interested in apprehending the thief in order to save his life than to recover the vehicle. But the thief, not realizing their intentions, fled from the very people who sought to help him.

I don't know if this story is true or not—sometimes truth is indeed stranger than fiction. But the story illustrates an important truth. So often we run from God in order to escape His punishment. But what we are actually doing is eluding His rescue.

God is omniscient. He knows all about us. He knows what we have

1

done in the past and will do in the future. The wondrous thing about God's love is that it never stops. He loves us the same today as He did yesterday, and His love for us will not change tomorrow. When we feel as though we have failed in life, God comes to us and raises up a banner of hope on our behalf: "Hope does not disappoint, because the love of God has been poured out within our hearts through the Holy Spirit who was given to us" (ROM. 5:5).

With this truth in mind, we must ask why so many people end up living less-than-productive lives. The answer lies in our ability to accept and apply a crucial truth to our hearts: it is God's unconditional love that changes us and brings lasting fulfillment. Once we understand and accept that there is no greater love than the love of God, we will be ready to take the first step toward living the extraordinary life.

What goals do you hope to achieve? What dream has God placed within your heart that you long to see become a reality? Despite your fears and insecurities, you can realize these longings. There is a way to live each day fulfilled, satisfied, and blessed.

Too many people are stuck in a rut, unable to pursue a better life. Maybe they are afraid of what they would find if they looked deep within themselves. Perhaps they fear failure. Even worse, they fear success. Particularly in Christian circles, we are taught to shrink from too much success. But false humility never makes a person more spiritual. God created each one of us in the brilliant image of His Son, Jesus Christ, and His power exists within us; we have only to move out of the way and let our Master bring it forth.

ABIDING IN CHRIST

Years ago, I fell victim to the trap of fretting, rushing, and striving. At the center of my life was the belief that to succeed in the Christian life, a person's focus must be set on Jesus Christ. However, I was working overtime to please God. Finally I came to a point of burnout. God used the testimony of Hudson Taylor to minister to me.

This great missionary to China came to a point of spiritual weariness. In a letter to his mother, Taylor wrote,

> My own position becomes continually more and more responsible, and my need greater of special grace to fill it, but I have continually to mourn that I follow at such a distance and learn so slowly to imitate my precious Master. I cannot tell you how I am buffeted sometimes by temptation. I never knew how bad a heart I had. Yet I do know that I love God and love His work, and desire to serve Him only in all things . . . Do pray for me. Pray that the Lord will keep me from sin, will sanctify me wholly, will use me more largely in His service.[1]

The verse God used to change Taylor's life was GALATIANS 2:20: "I have been crucified with Christ; and it is no longer I who live, but Christ lives in me; and the life which I now live in the flesh I live by faith in the Son of God, who loved me and gave Himself up for me."

When a person accepts Christ as his Savior, his old sin nature is crucified. But God does not leave him in a crucified state. This is why Jesus Christ came. He died for our sins and now offers us new life that is abundant and fulfilling. When Hudson Taylor exchanged his sinful, earthbound life for the life of Christ, he was set free to experience all the goodness of God.

JOHN 15 became a reality to him and, through my reading his story, to me also: "Abide in Me, and I in you. As the branch cannot bear fruit of itself unless it abides in the vine, so neither can you unless you abide in Me. I am the vine, you are the branches; he who abides in Me and I in him, he bears much fruit; for apart from Me you can do nothing" (vv. 4–5).

The person who abides in the Lord lives not for himself but for Jesus Christ. As I meditated on these verses, I discovered that it was *not* my responsibility to strive for anything. My part was to submit my life to God and allow Him to live His life through me. At my discovery, an enormous weight was lifted and removed from my life. Peace unlike anything I'd ever known filled my life. The energy and strength that ran through the life of Jesus Christ became mine.

In abiding, we discover that God takes our thoughts and conforms them to His will and purpose. He sharpens our talents, purifies our minds, and prepares us for service in His kingdom. Our treasures—the things we hold dear—become offerings of praise and worship to Him. Feelings of resentment and bitterness fade because His love and forgiveness are ours to experience and enjoy. We can rest because God is in control of all things. In essence, He refocuses our spiritual eyesight to see only Him and not the things that make us feel fearful and unsure.

When we go back to the basics of our faith, all we do, say, and believe is a result of our love and trust in Jesus Christ. We can make the most of the opportunities He provides because we know that He has a plan and purpose for our existence (JER. 29:11).

I often encourage those in our congregation to write a mission statement for their lives, and you should do the same. Ask God to show you how He wants you to live your life. You are never too young or too old to set goals with His mission in mind. Each person who dedicates his or her life to God is given a valuable role to play in His kingdom.

We may not realize the impact of our lives on others. However, God does. He is looking for willing vessels; He will do the rest. Ask Him, "Lord, how do You want me to invest the rest of my life?" It may involve something other than your vocation—a job may or may not represent your life purpose. We are called to be Christ's disciples in *every* area of life. Peter, Andrew, and John spent three years with the Savior. During that time, Jesus laid a basic foundation for their lives. There was an eternal definition to their lives because they walked and talked with the Savior each day. One of the basics of the Christian life is the act of spending time with Christ. When our lives and hearts are focused on Him, we will discover His purpose.

Often people become entrapped by the question, *What does God want me to do?* His Word says, "Trust in the LORD with all your heart and do not lean on your own understanding. In all your ways acknowledge Him, and He will make your paths straight" (PROV. 3:5–6). When you commit your way to God, He will place you in the position He wants you to occupy. It is a matter of simple, basic trust in God.

Never feel guilty for returning to the basics of your faith. Christian leaders have told me that when they find themselves at a point of dryness, they return to the basics of their faith in God. They take extra time to be alone with the Lord and listen for His encouragement. They practice being in His presence, even though they may be in a crowd of people.

A peace and a rest abide deep within the lives of those who let go of selfish desires long enough to experience the reality of God's goodness. Learning to abide instead of striving teaches you to place your trust in Someone who knows much more than you do about life and what is to come. Once you have experienced God's goodness, you will never want to return to a life of striving and self-effort. You will want to know more about your Savior and how your life can more effectively reflect His love and grace to others.

Matthew left everything to follow Jesus. The money box that held the taxes he collected had been his source of financial support for years. When Jesus called to him, he left everything. His time became God's time. It was no longer his own. What is your greatest desire? The Bible says that where your treasure is, your heart is also (MATT. 6:21).

After his discovery of the abiding life, Hudson Taylor wrote to his sister,

> The last month or more has been perhaps the happiest of my life; and I long to tell you a little of what the Lord has done for my soul. I do not know how far I may be able to make myself intelligible about it, for there is nothing new or strange or wonderful—and yet, all is new! In a word, "Whereas once I was blind, now I see." The sweetest part . . . is the rest which full identification with Christ brings. I am no longer anxious about anything, as I realize this; for He, I know, is able to carry out His will, and His will is mine. It makes no matter where He places me or how. This is rather for Him to consider than for me; for in the easiest positions He must give me His grace, and in the most difficult His grace is sufficient.[2]

Even though Hudson Taylor came to realize this great truth, his life was not free of trouble. Trials will come, but we must remember they are limited by God's omnipotence. When they do hit, He is with us in the midst of the wind and fury, the pain and suffering. There is never a time He leaves us to work things out on our own.

It is possible that you have been a Christian for years, but for some reason you are experiencing unreality with God. Ask the Lord to surface anything in your life that you need to surrender to Him. Your devotion and trust may have drifted. If that is the case, you need to address this first. Pray for God to renew your heart and refresh your spirit as you seek His counsel for your life.

If you have never received Christ as your Savior, you can exchange your old way of living for a new, victorious life. Tell Him that you want His life to be yours, and accept His death on the cross as sufficient payment for your sins. In so doing, you agree with Him that there is nothing you can do in your own strength to save yourself. It is through faith in God's Son that you are saved.

Once you have done this, you are ready to begin with the basics of the Christian faith—becoming a wise steward of your time, thoughts, talents, and treasures. Commit your desires, hopes, and dreams to God, and you will be amazed at the way He works everything together for your good and His glory.

OUR GREATEST PRIVILEGE

Of all the people you have met, which one do you feel most privileged to know? Is it some athlete or accomplished performer? Perhaps it is an admired coworker, precious grandparent, or godly friend. As special as such people might be, our supreme privilege is to know God.

A personal relationship with the sovereign Lord of the universe is an unparalleled opportunity and eternal treasure. Nothing else in human existence—no experience, friendship, or knowledge—can bring you lasting peace, joy, fulfillment, or security. Nor can anything else offer eternal life.

The apostle Paul recognized that even the most highly esteemed achievements pale in comparison to the "surpassing value of knowing Christ" (PHIL. 3:8); his consuming desire was to know the God who had transformed his very being. In contrast, many people go through life without ever knowing Him. They reach the end of their days as unbelievers, having failed to discover the purpose for which they were created and missing the blessings God had in store. What a tragedy!

Why do people fail to know their Creator? To begin with, many individuals live in darkness, unaware that there is one true God whom Jesus Christ came to reveal. For some reason, they were never exposed to the preaching of the gospel—a problem more prevalent perhaps in non-Christian societies, but in no way limited to them; it is even common inside the walls of many churches.

Another reason is lack of interest in God. With cell phones, televisions, radios, and computers, we are overwhelmed with information, but no wiser than we were without them. Convinced that access to information equals knowledge, we often replace true wisdom with trivia. Even if diplomas cover your walls, unless you know Jesus Christ as your personal Savior, you are ignorant about the most important thing in life—you cannot know God without knowing Christ (JOHN 14:7).

Knowing God involves a cost, and some people are simply unwilling to pay the price. Too often, once people get saved, they are no longer interested in investing time in Scripture and prayer to know the Father more deeply. But for any relationship to grow, we must spend time communicating, listening, and making an effort to understand more about the other person.

Do you really want to know God? The way to do that is by knowing Christ: receive Him as your Savior, who paid your sin-debt in full. Then accept His invitation to spend time in private conversation—He wants your undivided attention for a little while.

GOD'S PURPOSE IS THAT YOU MANIFEST THE LIFE OF JESUS CHRIST

Fulfillment is the result of God's presence living within you through His indwelling Holy Spirit. All that you do in life should reflect His goodness and mercy. But how do you reach a point of true fulfillment?

First, you must realize that fulfillment is not a matter of position or power. It is a matter of loving God and allowing Him to love you. All you need in order to be fulfilled is Jesus Christ living within you. You are God's beloved child—an heir to His throne. There is no higher calling than this, and there is no greater position than the place you hold in His family. Truthfully, as a Christian, you have both authority and power. Although at times life may seem to have lost its sense of excitement and you may no longer hopefully anticipate the future, you should not settle for less. You can be fulfilled right now.

Before His death, Jesus assured His disciples that He would never leave them: "I will not leave you as orphans; I will come to you" (JOHN 14:18). His promise applies to followers today as much as it did to His companions. Three days after the Crucifixion, He rose from the grave. Today He lives within those who pray a simple prayer like this: "Father, I confess that I need the Savior. I have sinned, and my life is empty and without hope. I know that the Lord Jesus is the hope of all humanity. I pray that You will forgive my sin and give me a fresh opportunity to live my life for You. I long to live life to the fullest, and I realize that this begins as I submit my life to You. I ask You to give me a new life. In Jesus' name I pray."

God designed your life for His glory. Even before you knew Him personally, He knew you intimately: "'For I know the plans that I have for you,' declares the LORD, 'plans for welfare and not for calamity to give you a future and a hope'" (JER. 29:11). When we surrender ourselves to God, we exchange our thoughts, feelings, and desires for new ones. Faith is the only way we can do this. By faith we believe that God is who He says He is and that He will do exactly what He has promised.

We can still reach our goals, overcome our failures, and enjoy success, but for a different reason. Instead of boasting about what we have achieved in our own capabilities, we can enjoy what God has given abundantly. Our lives become reflections of His life and love rather than a checklist of human accomplishments.

Submit yourself to God. Fulfillment comes only when you decide to love God and give Him all of yourself. This does not mean that you settle for second best or stop doing what you have been trained to do. Instead, you come to a point where you ask God to use you to the fullest so that others will come to know Him and experience His forgiveness and unconditional love. Those who have never discovered the wondrous joy that comes from loving and serving God have yet to experience His eternal fulfillment.

God has a great plan for your life—a life that is exceptional. When you trust and seek only Him, He will teach you how to live above your circumstances. Each one of us has been blessed with a spiritual gift to be used for God's glory and work. Yielding to Him is the first step in the process of discovering that gift and the wondrous purpose for your life.

Your understanding of *who* you are is the rudder that directs nearly everything you do. You must believe the truth about who God says you are: a genuine masterpiece. Knowing who you are and who you were created to be will transform performance-based notions of self-worth into a certainty upheld by God's infinite love. Scripture tells us that if anyone is in Christ, he is a new creation; the old has gone, and the new has come (2 COR. 5:17).

You are the creation of God's hands—His imprint is upon you, and He wants you to be a reflection of His glory and character: "We all, with unveiled face, beholding as in a mirror the glory of the Lord, are being transformed into the same image from glory to glory, just as from the Lord, the Spirit" (2 COR. 3:18).

He wants you to understand why you were created (and then re-created through Christ) as well as your purpose in this life. When you understand how beloved you are and the greatness of your purpose, you will be energized to live for God through His power.

Your identity is secure because of who lives inside you, not because of what you do. Few of us, if any, seek a mundane existence. Instead, we long to experience life in a grand way. The glut of reality TV shows is genuine evidence of people craving something bigger than the ordinary lives they lead. Because we want to grow emotionally and intellectually, we constantly seek new ways to expand our vision and enjoy life more. However, extreme sports challenges, exotic vacations, and hedonistic thrills promise more than they can deliver.

There is only one antidote for spiritual thirst. God also wants us to experience permanent fulfillment. He created us for excellence, and from His perspective, our lives represent infinite possibilities. No matter how many wrong turns we take, God knows how to redirect our lives and set us back on the right track. He is the One who extends opportunity after opportunity to us. In other words, He is the God of the second, third, fourth, and infinite chances.

THE HOUND OF HEAVEN

Poet Francis Thompson, a former opium addict, wrote about his encounter with the Lord. He described God as a "hound of heaven" who chased him down every street and alley of his life and mind until he surrendered to Christ and finally found peace. If you run from God, He will follow; if you avoid Him, He will pursue; if you hide, He will find you.

God's message to us is always profound and personal, and it deserves our complete attention. Why? He has charted a perfect course for our lives. Knowing the future completely, He sees when our plans do not align with His. When we begin to wander from His course, He will go to great lengths to get our attention.

Because we are Christians, it is incumbent upon us to be savvy travelers, alert to our Master's voice as we journey through life. We must walk in the Spirit, which means being receptive and responsive to God's instruction, no matter how He chooses to speak. And we must know how to distinguish between His voice and the others that vie for our attention—the opinions of our peers, rebellious attitudes, or lust for the world.

All too often, the Lord's wisdom is muffled by the clamor of daily life. Sometimes we start out with God's agenda but get so far ahead of Him that we can no longer hear His voice. Preferring to do things our own way, we lose contact with our only true Guide.

God's objective in communicating with us is that we become conformed to the image of His Son and express His love to the world. He speaks primarily in four ways—through His Word, through His Holy Spirit, through another person, and through the circumstances in our lives.

Ideally we should be so attuned to His voice that we hear as soon as He speaks. If you have been a Christian long enough, you have probably experienced this—when the Holy Spirit prompted you in the middle of work or another activity, you sensed it right away and knew exactly what to do. Unfortunately we are not always spiritually "tuned in." For such situations, God has a number of ways to get our attention.

A RESTLESS SPIRIT

One of the simplest ways God gets our attention is by making us restless. When King Ahasuerus was unable to sleep, he ordered that the royal record books be read. As a result, he discovered his life had been saved by Esther's uncle. In wanting to honor Mordecai, the king unwittingly set in motion a chain of events that caused Haman's planned annihilation of the Jews to backfire (EST. 6–7). The Jewish nation was spared because the king was alert when God gave him a restless spirit.

If you experience a restlessness deep within—something you sense but cannot quite identify—the wise thing to do is stop and pray, "Lord, are You trying to say something to me?" God does not work the same way in everyone's life, but I believe His primary method for getting my attention is by giving me a restlessness to show I need a change of direction. As I reread my old journal entries, a pattern emerges—every single time God was about to move me from one pastorate to another, I would become very restless for a few months. This is a very gentle method that God uses to correct our course.

A SPOKEN WORD

A second way that God gets our attention is by a word spoken through someone else. Wanting to give Eli the priest a message, the Lord woke young Samuel by calling his name (1 SAM. 3:4–8). At first, the boy did not realize it was the voice of his Lord. Eli had to instruct him to listen carefully because God had a special message for Samuel (v. 9). Young

Samuel did not know the Lord as deeply as did Eli, so God used the priest to pass along a word of encouragement to the boy. In a similar way, God also had Eli's attention for the forthcoming message He would deliver through Samuel (vv. 11–18).

AN UNUSUAL BLESSING

A third way that God speaks is the method most people prefer: by blessing us in an unusual way. The blessing might be related to spiritual growth, finances, home, work, or health. God does not always choose this method. For those who turn away and refuse to depend on Him, a lavish blessing would likely result in greater independence and self-centeredness—God would be totally ignored. If you are an overly self-sufficient person, be aware that God may use some other method to get your focus onto Him. But remember that no matter which method He uses to get your attention, it is always an expression of His love.

UNANSWERED PRAYER

The fourth method is sometimes the hardest: God answers even the most fervent prayers by denying our request when our desires are not in sync with His. David implored God to save his infant son's life, but the child died (2 SAM. 12:16–18). It is important to point out that God loves everybody equally, but He has different purposes for each life. The child's death was used to get David's attention in an extreme situation involving the nation's leader who deliberately acted against the will of God.

Sin is one reason the Lord will use unanswered prayer to get our attention. Even if the prayer itself is in line with God's will—perhaps even exactly what He wants to do—the Lord may close the doors of heaven and refuse to answer that prayer as a way of forcing us to examine ourselves. When necessary, God uses drastic measures, but we must never take it upon ourselves to pass judgment against fellow believers—that task belongs solely to the Lord.

DISAPPOINTMENT

God will sometimes use disappointment to get our attention. In NUMBERS 14, the nation of Israel was poised at the border of the promised land, ready to take possession of it. However, the spy "committee" voted ten to two against possessing what God promised to give His people in battle. The Scripture describes His judgment upon the nation for their unbelief. The people acknowledged that they had indeed sinned, but now changed their minds and desired to enter the land. However, the Lord said no—it was too late. Although there must have been a tremendous sense of disappointment and mourning, God certainly had their attention. It was for their benefit that He revealed the error of not trusting Him. In a similar way, God today allows setbacks to keep us from charting our own course rather than doing His will.

EXTRAORDINARY CIRCUMSTANCES

Sometimes God will use bizarre or unusual circumstances to get us to stop and listen. Moses saw a bush that was on fire but not consumed (EX. 3:2). As he approached to investigate, the Lord spoke to him from the flame. You and I must learn to look for the presence of God in every circumstance. He leaves His footprints and handiwork all around us, and we will recognize them more often when we are watchful.

DEFEAT

Another method God uses is defeat. Following the Lord's stunning victory over Jericho, the Israelites approached the small town of Ai with overconfidence, and they neglected to fight in God's strength or with His military plan (JOSH. 7). God got Joshua's attention by letting him fail miserably. But notice there is a big difference between failing and being a failure. A terrible defeat may prove to be the greatest stepping-stone to success when we are wise enough to ask, "Lord, what are You saying?"

FINANCIAL TROUBLES

In the book of Judges, "every man did what was right in his own eyes," and the nation fell into idolatry and disobedience (JUDG. 17:6). God brought judgment through the Midianites, who devastated the land, leaving neither livestock nor possessions. At what point did the Israelites finally cry out to the Lord? When He took away every material belonging and drove the people into caves and mountains to hide and save their lives (JUDG. 6:2–6). God knew exactly what it would take to get their attention. After they turned to Him, He delivered them from their oppressors and blessed them.

TRAGEDY, SICKNESS, AND AFFLICTION

Although we must never look at someone else's situation and presume why God allowed a calamity, we should regard our tragedies and afflictions as reasons to inquire of the Lord, "What are You trying to say?" When King Hezekiah became prideful, God used illness to alert him to the problem (2 CHRON. 32:24). Similarly, when Saul of Tarsus was persecuting Christians, he was stricken with blindness—then the Lord certainly had his attention (ACTS 9:3–5)!

At any given moment, God knows exactly where you are in your journey and precisely what it will take to get your attention. So be alert; notice if any of God's methods are occurring—or recurring—in your life. Ask Him what He wants to tell you, and then listen, not simply to hear, but to obey. Jesus said, "Behold, I stand at the door, and knock: if any man hear my voice, and open the door, I will come in to him, and will sup with him, and he with me" (REV. 3:20 KJV). Because of His great love for you and His desire to give you a hope and a future, God is always reaching toward you.

SUGGESTED BIBLE READING

ROMANS 5:5; GALATIANS 2:20; JOHN 15:4–5;
JEREMIAH 29:11; PROVERBS 3:5–6; MATTHEW 6:21;
PHILIPPIANS 3:7–8; JOHN 14:7, 18; 2 CORINTHIANS
3:18; 5:17; and ESTHER 6–7.

PRAYER

Father, I surrender my life to You today, knowing that
my works will not gain me entrance into the kingdom
of God. I trust solely in the blood of Your Son, Jesus
Christ, for my strength. Give me a desire for You and
for Your Word, and reveal to me the strongholds that
prevent me from complete surrender. Amen.

JOURNAL QUESTIONS

- What does it mean to be "crucified with Christ"?

_____

_____

_____

_____

- What can we learn through the story of Esther about God's plan in our lives?

_____

_____

_____

_____

- What steps can you take today to surrender completely to God?

_____

_____

_____

_____

Can you trust God enough to fully surrender to Him? Absolutely.
Visit *www.InTouch.org* today to see why God is worthy
of your complete confidence.

PRINCIPLE 2

GOD'S GRACE IS THE STARTING POINT

When our ministry began an outreach to Russia, I took a trip to that formerly oppressed nation. While there, I decided to visit Vladimir Lenin's tomb. However, at that time, the lines were so long that I was forced to leave without seeing the burial chamber of the toppled dictator.

Thirty years later, I returned to the site, and there were no lines—no anxious tourists clamoring to see the remains of a fallen man. I made my way through a row of guards and stood directly in front of a sign that read, "No talking."

As I gazed upon Lenin's lifeless body, which was encased in an airtight glass casket, I felt a sense of despair. There, lying in front of me, was the corpse of a man renowned for creating mass terror and the first concentration camps ever built on the continent.

Lenin is probably known most for the merciless imposition of his extreme ideas on an entire nation. He made terror and bloodshed the hallmarks of his rule, paving the way for dictators who followed, like

Stalin, Hitler, and Pol Pot. All of these men left their people with shattered dreams and no hope of a life beyond the dismal ones created by their tormentors.

I walked out of that place and stood for a moment, taking in the cold winter air. Immediately my thoughts went to another tomb—one that was empty. But the crowds were still coming.

I thought back to a time when I had visited the Savior's grave on a trip to Israel. I had waited until everyone left the area, then fell on my face before God. The stillness of the moment did not demand my silence. Instead, it demanded my praise and worship.

There is a profound difference between these two tombs. One still contains a lifeless form; the other is empty. One man started a revolution that led to depravity, destruction, and death; the other Man began a revolution that continues today, a revolution of hope and eternal life—one that sets captives free from the bondage of spiritual darkness and opens the door to unconditional love, forgiveness, and grace.

CHRIST PAID THE PRICE FOR YOUR SINS

Every once in a while I hear somebody casually say, "Well, I guess I'm just going to hell when I die." No one in his right mind should speak so carelessly! Everyone is going to spend eternity in either heaven or hell—there is no escape. There is not a single verse of Scripture that says that your life becomes void once you have died. Let me say this: it would be better never to have been born than to die without Christ!

To all of us who know Jesus as our personal Savior, God has entrusted us with the most awesome and glorious message, unmatched by anything else in history. That message is simple: our unconditionally loving heavenly Father sent His only begotten Son, Jesus, into this wicked, vile, sinful world to die on a cruel Roman cross. There, Christ paid the sin-debt of all humanity in order to atone for our sin and reconcile us to God. When you receive Christ by faith as your personal Savior, your eternal destiny is transformed. One moment lost, and the next moment saved. Formerly headed for hell; now with a home in heaven.

THE RESURRECTION—REASON TO REJOICE

I remember several years ago standing behind the curtain during our church's Easter passion play. At the end of each performance, I stepped out and explained how trusting the Lord Jesus Christ as one's personal Savior can save a person from sin. Onstage, Jesus had just risen, and the disciples were running back to look inside the tomb. I got so caught up in their excitement that, for a brief moment, I wanted to go out on stage amid all those actors dressed like people who lived two thousand years ago and look inside the empty tomb.

Some ask why we celebrate the Resurrection. The main reason is that Jesus Christ, our Lord and Savior, is alive. No other religious leader who ever lived and died can make such a claim. For that matter, every single leader or celebrity who has died—political, academic, or artistic—remains buried just like Lenin unless his or her body has somehow been removed by man. Their tombs are often honored as places of national or religious pride.

But of what do we Christians boast? We celebrate an empty tomb because the One we love, the One we follow, the One we serve is no longer there. Now, if Jesus Christ rose from the dead, where is He? Scripture tells us precisely where He is: He is seated at the right hand of God.

When we pray, He intercedes with the Father on our behalf (HEB. 7:25). Moreover, we know from JOHN 14 that Jesus is preparing a place for you and me in heaven, and one day, we will be with Him there (VV. 2–3). In the meantime, He is arranging all the events necessary for His return.

According to 1 JOHN 2:1–2, Jesus Christ is also our Advocate. You see, when the Son of God saved us, He knew we would not live perfect lives—He knew we would sin against Him. So He stands between us and the Father to present our case. This defense is based not merely upon our confession and repentance for the forgiveness of sin, but upon the fact that Jesus Himself laid down His life and paid our sin-debt in full. When He went to the cross, He died a substitutionary, sacrificial death on our behalf. So we can be absolutely confident that our sins are totally forgiven. Salvation has nothing to do with our behavior, but it has everything to do with the grace of God, the love of God, the goodness of God, the mercy of God, and the blood of Jesus Christ.

The resurrection of Jesus Christ has given us a very definite purpose for being alive. He has saved us for the purpose of reflecting His life in our work, our ways, our words, and our walk. That is why you and I are the body of Christ. He is looking through our eyes, hearing through our ears, speaking through our voices, and helping through our hands. Having created us for Himself, He desires that you and I walk in holiness and righteousness before Him. We are to be Christ's representatives, pointing people to Him and reflecting His light to a dark world that desperately needs Him.

The Resurrection provides assurance, confidence, and boldness for us. It determines where we are in life, where we are headed, and where we are going to end up—in the very presence of the living God instead of eternally separated from Him.

REVELATION 21:27 tells us that no one can enter heaven except "those whose names are written in the Lamb's book of life." How do you get your name inscribed in that book? By accepting the Lamb of God— the person of Jesus Christ—as your personal Savior, based on the fact that He died on the cross, paying your sin-debt in full. Three days after He was buried, He rose again. Believe it . . . and celebrate!

GRACE IS THE ONLY MEANS TO SALVATION; YOU CAN'T EARN IT

I want to share with you a life-changing experience I had about twenty years ago. I was in my late forties and working hard as a pastor, but I knew something was lacking in my walk with the Lord. I began searching my heart to see if anything was hindering my relationship with God, but I was left with only the keen awareness of the void in my heart.

When this tension in my spiritual life came to a head, I called four of my closest friends. They agreed to meet with me and help me discover what was missing so that I could find peace with God. The first night of our meeting, I talked for more than eight hours, telling them everything about myself. Later, I sat up most of the night filling seventeen legal-sized pages with more intimate details of my life.

The following morning, I revealed every piece of personal information to my friends. After the group reflected upon what I had said, one member asked me to elaborate on the death of my father, who had died when I was nine months old. After I finished, he told me to close my eyes. Then he said, "Picture this: your father has just picked you up in his arms and is holding you. What do you feel?"

That meeting with my friends took place decades ago, but I remember it vividly. I cried. I felt warm, loved, and secure. I had never felt the amazing depth of my heavenly Father's love until then. I was saved at twelve years of age, but that meeting with my friends was the first time I felt with all my heart that God truly loved me—not as a distant, impersonal deity, but as my loving, heavenly Father.

Accepting the incredibly expansive love of God is not easy. For years I was convinced that the distance I felt from God must be linked to some sin in my life. I prayed incessantly for forgiveness, even trying to find sins that weren't there. Many Christians live this way, harboring feelings of shame and self-doubt that have more to do with their fear of intimacy than with reality.

Many people know they are saved but have never discovered the true joy and contentment of being children of God. One of the primary reasons Paul wrote to the believers in Colossae was to express the freedom that was available through Jesus Christ. False teachers had entered their fellowship and taught that while it was right to accept Jesus as the Messiah, one must also live under the regulations of the Mosaic Law.

The burden was too great for the young church; its people lost their joy and fell into various forms of bondage. People today fall into the same trap when they attempt to demonstrate their Christianity through submission to human rules rather than allegiance to God alone. This is not the way of freedom in Christ. We cannot attest to God's work of grace while living under the bondage of the law. Completeness is found only in Jesus, not in abiding by prescribed rules or regulations.

Paul wrote,

In Him all the fullness of Deity dwells in bodily form, and in Him you have been made complete, and He is the head over all rule and authority; and in Him you were also circumcised with a circumcision made without hands, in the removal of the body of the flesh by the circumcision of Christ; having been buried with Him in baptism, in which you were also raised up with Him through faith in the working of God, who raised Him from the dead.

When you were dead in your transgressions and the uncircumcision of your flesh, He made you alive together with Him, having forgiven us all our transgressions, having canceled out the certificate of debt consisting of decrees against us, which was hostile to us; and He has taken it out of the way, having nailed it to the cross. When He had disarmed the rulers and authorities, He made a pub-

lic display of them, having triumphed over them through Him.
(COL. 2:9–15)

All we will ever need is found in Jesus. When we accept Him as our Savior, we are given a new spirit—one empowered by the Holy Spirit. We can understand spiritual truth because the Spirit of God renews our minds.

Paul told us, "If anyone is in Christ, he is a new creature; the old things passed away; behold, new things have come" (2 COR. 5:17). Christ's dwelling within us makes us sufficient and adequate for all things. God has regenerated our spirits. We are partakers of His divine nature, and it is no longer our nature to sin.

This does not mean, however, that we are perfect or will never sin again; it does not mean that when we abide in close fellowship with Christ, sin loses its appeal. Even though we are new creatures spiritually, our bodies are unchanged. God has given us certain natural appetites that are both normal and essential. Often, when we try to satisfy these appetites in our own strength, we yield to sinful desires. God wants us to understand our position as believers—we are totally complete in the Lord, who has promised to meet all of our needs within His perfect timing.

Every person carries perceptions acquired throughout life—particularly those that were instilled in childhood. When we reach adulthood and are no longer dependent on our parents, we should see clearly that our spirits need redemption—we ought to realize our deep, abiding need for a Savior. If we ask Jesus Christ to come into our lives, He will; genuine deliverance can be ours.

This process is both wonderful and challenging. There still remains a struggle. We have a new nature that no longer corresponds with our old way of doing things. A conflict erupts between serving God and yielding to the desires of the flesh.

In order to triumph over the flesh, you must understand your true identity in Christ. If you begin your Christian walk by thinking that you still have an old sin nature, plan to battle temptation the rest of your life. Sin is easier to yield to when we think we cannot help what we do or feel. We begin to tell ourselves it is just our old carnal nature coming through. Likewise, if you believe that God merely patched you up at the point of salvation, you will spend the rest of your life dealing with discouragement, doubt, and defeat.

With this mentality, we miss the radical truth of salvation; we overlook the truth of God's power in our lives. The moment you are saved, your sin nature dies and Jesus Christ abides in you. You have a new nature in Christ—one of obedience, submission, love, loyalty, and devotion to God. Christ enables you to live without submitting to sin.

When we go through baptismal waters, we proclaim the truth that we have died to our old sin nature and have been reborn in Jesus Christ (ROM. 6:1–11). We are new creatures in Him, not partially but completely. We have been raised with Christ and are seated in the heavenly places with Him.

Paul told us that the old things have passed away. All things are now new. That includes our spirits, our natures, our lives—every part of us. Many of us have a hard time accepting this truth. Often it is more natural to harbor guilt about past wrongs, but God says He has forgiven us of our transgressions and canceled our certificate of debt (COL. 2:13). Christ has canceled all judgment against us as well as condemnation of sin. They were nailed to the cross at Calvary.

We no longer have a sin-debt. We don't have to pay the price for our sins. Jesus paid it in full once and for all. Not only did God cancel our sin, He took it away—erased it through the sacrificial death of Jesus Christ. That is why the apostle Peter wrote, "He Himself bore our sins in His body on the cross, so that we might die to sin and live to righteousness" (1 PETER 2:24).

We do not receive forgiveness through confession or repentance. The only way we receive forgiveness is through the shed blood of the Lord Jesus Christ. It is God's personal gift of grace toward us.

When you confess your sins to God, you acknowledge and agree with Him that your life is not in keeping with His Word, will, or plan. Repentance signals a change in thinking. It shows that God's Spirit has convicted you of a particular sin and that you have chosen to turn away from it.

We cannot lead a sinful life and remain in right fellowship with God. Although He will never stop loving us, our disobedience invites God's discipline. Just as parents who love their children correct them when they are wrong, God disciplines us when we choose to disobey Him.

God, who is holy and righteous, has chosen to express His love for us through His Son. His love is genuine, undeserved, and unconditional. You can release all the guilt you have been carrying for years by accepting the complete forgiveness that is rightfully yours through Jesus Christ.

The truth is that many people miss God's very best because they refuse to remove the chains of guilt and sin from their lives. Each day they try to make it through life the best they can. Sunday after Sunday, they pray that the pastor will say something to help them bear the guilt they harbor. God wants all of us to rest in the liberty purchased by the blood of His Son, Jesus Christ.

When Jesus rose from the dead, He conquered every single power in opposition to Him not merely at that time, but forever: "Christ also died for sins once for all, the just for the unjust, so that He might bring us to God, having been put to death in the flesh, but made alive in the spirit; in which also He went and made proclamation to the spirits now in prison" (1 PETER 3:18–19).

Through His resurrection, Jesus proclaimed His sovereignty over all demonic powers. Satan and his forces are forever in subjection to Christ's rule and reign. That means nothing can touch your life apart from the permissive will of God. We have been released and liberated. Jesus, like a commanding general, walked into the Holy of Holies in absolute and total triumph over every single power and authority. Nothing is equal to the Holy Spirit who abides in each of us (JOHN 15:5). Jesus Christ in you is your hope of glory (COL. 1:27).

We have a new nature, a new sense of liberty, a new freedom in His forgiveness. We have a new standard of conduct that we can keep through the power of the Holy Spirit.

Jesus cried out from the cross and said, "It is finished!" (JOHN 19:30). There is nothing you can add to your salvation or the freedom He has given you. There is nothing you can do to make yourself more saved, more forgiven. When Christ atoned for your sins, He erased the slate and marked your account "paid in full" and credited your ledger with all the benefits of being His beloved child. All you have to do to experience the extraordinary life is to begin making withdrawals by faith.

The Christian life is an expression of God's grace rather than a checklist of dos and don'ts. It is an overflow of Jesus Christ. That is what Christianity is all about—freedom to enjoy the life God has given us, and freedom to share this truth with others.

Jesus Christ, through the power of the Holy Spirit within you, will empower you to do whatever God requires of you (1 THESS. 5:24). You can find all the strength, hope, and love that you will ever need in Christ when you live and abide in His resurrection power.

Unless you have trusted Jesus as your Savior, you have never experienced true freedom. By placing your trust in Him as your personal Savior and accepting what He has offered you through the mercy of His grace, you will know freedom from the bondage of sin. Your life will be made new: the old will be cut away, and you will be made fully alive.

God made the decision to love us long before He shaped the foundation of this world. He knew our deepest need even before it existed. It was the need for a Savior. Have you ever wondered why God chose to come to earth as a baby—helpless and seemingly unprotected? The answer lies within His wisdom and desire for you to know and experience His intimate love. The apostle Paul wrote, "Just as He chose us in Him before the foundation of the world, that we would be holy and blameless before Him. In love He predestined us to adoption as sons through Jesus Christ to Himself, according to the kind intention of His will" (EPH. 1:4–5).

Although His law demanded payment for sin, the heavenly Father knew that the payment was far too great for us. Only God in His infinite wisdom is capable of providing the atonement needed to eradicate our sin.

ETERNAL SECURITY MATTERS

Every year during Easter, we focus our thoughts on the sacrifice of Jesus Christ at Calvary. From His atonement springs our blessed assurance of salvation and eternal life. Many people who trust Christ as their Savior know they are saved but are not quite certain about eternal security, the work of God that assures salvation is permanent. They believe salvation can somehow be lost through wrong actions or a voluntary choice to forfeit it.

Does it really matter if we believe in eternal security? The answer is yes! Eternity is one of God's promises, and He wants His children to be confident about their guaranteed future with Him. That is why John declared, "These things I have written to you who believe in the name of the Son of God, so that you may know that you have eternal life" (1 JOHN 5:13). In fact, not one Scripture passage in any way limits the saving power of Christ's sacrificial, substitutionary death.

The Bible teaches that when we receive Jesus Christ as Savior, we unequivocally *have* eternal life. This God-given assurance influences every aspect of our faith. Eternal security is a foundational cornerstone for effective and godly service in the power of the Holy Spirit. A believer who is sure of eternity is not working to get something from God, but is diligently serving Him out of devotion.

The promise of heaven affects our understanding of repentance and forgiveness. We repent of our sins in order to receive Christ as our Savior. That is, we change our thinking about sinful behavior and confess our helplessness to God. Because of that repentance, we receive forgiveness and are "saved"—our relationship with God starts right then and continues without interruption. Thereafter, the acts of repentance and confession serve a different purpose. They are not necessary for gaining our forgiveness because we already possess a full measure. Instead, repentance makes right our fellowship with Christ.

Our assurance of salvation depends upon eternal security. If salvation is based upon *anything* other than the completed work of Jesus Christ on the cross, then we find ourselves on shaky ground. Some believers attempt to involve themselves in the salvation process by good works or right behavior; such people are prone to doubts about eternity because they feel they must *earn* God's goodwill and heaven. Grace is a gift (EPH. 2:8–9). If we add a single work requirement to salvation, then it is no longer a gift; it is payment for services rendered. That is simply not how God works in the life of the believer.

What's more, we are eternally secure in our Lord. There's not a single verse anywhere in Scripture indicating our salvation lasts only for a season. Notice what the Bible says: the Lord gives believers *eternal* life, and we will *never perish* (JOHN 10:28, emphasis added); we are "*sealed* for the day of redemption" (EPH. 4:30, emphasis added), which means the ultimate day when God calls us home. We are assured that no one can snatch us out of God's hand (JOHN 10:27–30).

So let me ask you a question: Do you think you have the power to take anything out of the hand of Omnipotence? Once you've trusted Jesus Christ as your Savior, you may have doubts or fears. You may rebel and sin against Him. But that in no way means you have lost your salvation. If it did imply such a thing, what could God possibly have meant by "I give eternal life to them, and they will *never* perish" (JOHN 10:28, emphasis added)? This isn't license for sin; this is reason to rejoice, to praise God, to walk holy before Him, and to obey Him. If Jesus had not risen from the grave, we might have reason to doubt our eternal security, but the fact that He was resurrected settles once and for all the truth of everything He said as well as the guarantee of everything He promised.

When you and I trusted Jesus as our Savior, we didn't receive just forgiveness of our sins; we received His very life. Through the Holy Spirit, Jesus is right now abiding inside us (JOHN 15:4) to help each believer live the Christian life (GAL. 2:20). He promised that He would not leave us as orphans, fending for ourselves, but instead, He would send us another Helper—the Holy Spirit—who would be with us forever, dwelling not only with us, but in us (JOHN 14:16).

That is a profound difference between believers and unbelievers: both experience life on earth, but we who believe look forward to an abundant life with our heavenly Father after we die. Jesus was, is, and always will be—He will live forever, and the eternal life He offers is likewise of infinite duration. In addition, He gives us the quality and nature of the life He Himself possesses—it is glorious, abundant, and indescribable. He has given us Himself.

If He has given us eternal life, will our bodies get old? Will our muscles weaken and our hair go gray? Yes, the body will change with time, but the soul and the spirit will mature and become stronger. Scripture tells us that Christians are going to live forever, but not in their earthly bodies. Every single believer is going to experience a bodily resurrection! We know this, not only because Christ Himself was resurrected, but also because He told us, "This is the will of Him who sent Me, that of all that He has given Me I lose nothing, but raise it up on the last day" (JOHN 6:39). If you belong to Christ, you are going to experience a physical bodily resurrection.

We read in HEBREWS 9:27 that "it is appointed for men to die once and after this comes judgment." Every single person will one day stand in the presence of Jesus Christ to give an account of his or her life. Scripture speaks of two coming resurrections, the first being "unto life," which guarantees reward to every believer (REV. 20:6). The other resurrection, which is reserved for all people who have rejected the Lord Jesus, is unto judgment and condemnation. It results in eternal separation from God, which the Bible calls the "second death" (REV. 20:11–15).

LIVING IN GRACE

Do you set rules and regulations for your life, but then judge yourself very harshly when you do not live up to your expectations? Do you feel close to the Lord when you are doing something religious, but distant when you are not? Many people today are living in this manner—they lack assurance that they have pleased God. The Bible says that you and I have been accepted by His grace, which can be defined as God's kindness toward us without consideration of any merit on our part.

In the Old Testament, the ark of the covenant—which symbolized God's presence—was kept in a secured place in the Tabernacle called "The Holy of Holies." Access to this divine place was permitted only once per year and was restricted to the high priest. The Israelite people never were able to get anywhere close to the ark. A personal relationship with God was unthinkable. Instead, their whole concept of relating to God involved living up to laws and achieving acceptance on the basis of performance. The forgiveness of their sin was based on a literal animal sacrifice.

Jesus came in order to die for our sins and be a permanent, one-time substitutionary sacrifice. Forgiveness was only part of the plan; He came also to initiate an entirely different lifestyle from what the people of God had been experiencing. On the day of His crucifixion, the veil hiding the ark of the covenant was split from top to bottom, symbolizing that God opened the door to an intimate relationship with Him. He has made it possible for us to talk directly to Him and know we are being heard. That change in relationship reflects the difference between grace and law.

Jesus' death and resurrection settled the basis of our acceptance once and for all. Though our conduct sometimes is not what it ought to be, we are nonetheless embraced as children of God. In order to enjoy the Christian life, we must view ourselves the way He sees us. People trying to live up to an impossible, invisible standard never know when they have pleased God. If life is a matter of rules and regulations, we will never have any peace or contentment.

We have a choice to make. We can set rules and live by legalistic domination, fear, and uncertainty, or we can choose to live in the wonderful acceptance that comes by the Cross. The life of grace—lived in His eternal grip—is available to everyone who will call upon Him.

THE TRANSFORMING GRACE OF GOD

The direction your life takes is affected by many things, such as the environment in which you live, the decisions you make, and the education you receive. But by far the most powerful influence in a believer's life is the transforming grace of God, which is His kindness toward you regardless of your worthiness and in spite of everything you deserve.

God's ultimate will is for every believer to be conformed to the likeness of His Son. His grace is responsible for your rebirth, and from that point it directs, moves, and influences you to become increasingly Christlike. In that way, you can say with the apostle Paul, "By the grace of God I am what I am" (1 COR. 15:10).

The apostle's life, in fact, is a powerful example of God's transforming grace. In PHILIPPIANS 3, Paul described how he once depended on his good works, nature, and conduct to gain acceptance before God. He did not originally understand there is only one way to be made acceptable in God's sight—by His grace. If good works and religious activity could in some way gain divine approval, Paul would never have written about his former vain attempts to win God's favor and his numerous faulty reasons for confidence: he was an observant Jew from a family of esteemed lineage (V. 5); he had zealously kept the law (V. 6); and he even tirelessly persecuted the Christian church, which he saw as an enemy of his faith (V. 6).

However, encountering the living Christ totally changed Paul, and he explained, "Whatever things were gain to me, those things I have [now] counted as loss" (PHIL. 3:7). He recognized that all of his human titles and achievements had absolutely no spiritual value. We, too, must realize we will never gain eternity by depending on anything we are or anything we do—salvation is unrelated to how much money we give, what excellent citizens we are, or how well we treat our families. It is by grace, and grace alone, that we are saved (EPH. 2:8–9).

Paul learned a valuable lesson: the only thing worth boasting about is the cross of Jesus Christ (GAL. 6:14). The Lord offered Himself as our substitutionary sacrifice, not because He saw anything in us worth saving, but because of His great love.

There are millions of people who sincerely but wrongly believe they will be acceptable to God based on how good they are. It grieves my heart to think they will die in ignorance, deceived by the false doctrine of working to earn the Lord's approval. By grace, Paul's thinking was corrected—he learned that everything he had counted as valuable was worthless. In this way, the worst enemy of Christianity became its greatest asset, its greatest motivator, and its dearest friend.

How did this change come about? Saul, the "Hebrew of Hebrews" committed to destroying anything related to Jesus Christ, was approaching Damascus. After a sudden flash of light, he fell to the ground blinded and heard Jesus saying, "Saul, Saul, why are you persecuting Me?" (ACTS 22:7–9). The future apostle learned that being critical of the church or Christians was equivalent to opposing Jesus Himself (MATT. 25:40), and that attacking the body of Christ meant putting oneself under the condemnation and judgment of God. But God's grace was about to transform Saul by giving him a new nature and a fresh start—his hostile, vengeful heart would abruptly be changed, and he would become the church's most powerful promoter. What made the difference was that Paul knew God was talking to him.

Is God talking to you? Is He asking you to do something you don't like or something you are afraid to do? You have free will, but God's voice is compelling. George Matheson's hymn describes grace this way: "O Love that will not let me go, I rest my weary soul in Thee." God knows that we are children, growing and being gradually conformed into His likeness— and He is patient, kind, and forgiving in the process of our transformation. Sometimes we may say, "No, God," but He has a profound way of adding a little more pressure and a little more "incentive" until we say, "I surrender, Father!"

Remember that it is out of His gentle love—not out of condemnation or chastisement—that our heavenly Father arranges our circumstances and challenges. What He asks us to do is always in our best interest and will be part of the process that conforms us to Christ's image. If you have repeatedly disobeyed Him, you need to ask some serious questions about your relationship with Him. This is how I see it: When it comes down to a final decision either for God or against Him, how can I say no to a Christ who loved me enough to die an excruciating, humiliating death in my place?

This grace that saves and transforms today is the same grace that changed Saul, the sinner, into Paul, the apostle. He acknowledged that God's grace was completely responsible for what he had become (1 COR. 15:10) and that was why he gloried in the Cross—he had no intentions of being saved, but God in His gracious love had wonderful plans for him.

Furthermore, Paul was an example to those around him as well as to future generations. God wanted all of us to know that if He can save a murderer like Paul and transform him completely, then He can save anyone.

Witnessing Paul's conversion makes us ask, "Who among us *cannot* be transformed by the grace of God?"

But don't be deceived by Paul's dramatic experience. I was saved at the age of twelve. I had been reading the Bible a great deal, and I understood that I needed God's forgiveness in my life. There was no flash of light; I simply stepped from the second pew, walked to the altar, and knelt down to pray. I came from a home where my mom read the Bible to me, so my getting saved at age twelve was somewhat normal and natural. But what I want to tell you is this: it took just as much grace to save me at twelve as it took to save Saul of Tarsus, the violent, hateful persecutor of the church. The Bible says all of us were dead in our trespasses and sins (EPH. 2:1). Jesus Christ is the way, the truth, and the life (JOHN 14:6). When we have Him, we are born again—and truly alive!

Once someone has been transformed from sinner to saint, four attitudes should become evident. First, we should exhibit true humility. Listen to how Paul described himself, the preeminent missionary and preacher of the gospel: "I am the least of the apostles, and not fit to be called an apostle, because I persecuted the church of God" (1 COR. 15:9). In the following verse, he credited God's grace for his transformation, and not anything he did. You will not find pride in the heart of a man or a woman who truly understands grace—that person will always point others to Christ, realizing that anything positive is due entirely to God.

The second attitude is one of obligation. Paul was so overwhelmed by the undeserved grace of God that he gave his life to fulfilling the mission the Lord assigned him. Paul acknowledged he was set aside before birth to be a preacher of the gospel (GAL. 1:15–16); he considered it an enormous privilege and gave himself wholeheartedly to the task. The apostle had so much gratitude for his salvation that he had to tell other people what had happened to him. You also have a message to share. Don't be quiet about it. It is wrong to keep God's love to yourself when there is a world of people hurting and dying in agony, sorrow, frustration, anger, disappointment, and despair.

A third thing we should demonstrate is a sense of dependence. Paul mentioned laboring "even more than all of them, yet not I, but the grace of God with me" (1 COR. 15:10). He was saying that he did not strive through his own efforts; the same grace, goodness, and power that transformed him are the same loving power at work in the believer's life every day. We do not have to depend on our own wisdom, abilities, talents, or strength. It is Christ in us who accomplishes things (PHIL. 4:13), and apart from Him, we can do nothing (JOHN 15:5).

One final attitude we should display is a spirit of absolute confidence. At the end of his life, Paul was able to say, "I have fought the good fight, I have finished the course, I have kept the faith" (2 TIM. 4:7). And Paul looked forward to receiving the crown of righteousness from the Lord Himself (V. 8).

Paul was an awesome example of the transforming power of God's grace, which took a man murderously opposed to Christ and changed him into the world's greatest missionary. He gave himself without reservation to proclaiming the gospel, and he was able to say that God's grace toward him "did not prove vain" (1 COR. 15:10). Has God poured His grace into your life? Don't let it be in vain—tell God how thankful you are . . . and tell others why.

SUGGESTED BIBLE READING

HEBREWS 7:25; 1 JOHN 2:1–2; REVELATION 21:27; COLOSSIANS 2:9–15; 1 PETER 2:24; 3:18–19; COLOSSIANS 1:27; JOHN 6:39; 10:27–30; 14:16; 15:4–5; 19:30; 1 THESSALONIANS 5:24; EPHESIANS 1:4–5; 2:1–9; 4:30; GALATIANS 1:15–16; 2:20; 6:14; REVELATION 20:11–15; PHILIPPIANS 3:7; 4:13; MATTHEW 25:4; 1 CORINTHIANS 15:9–10; and 2 TIMOTHY 4:7.

PRAYER

Dear heavenly Father, thank You for the gift of eternal life through the death of Your Son, Jesus Christ. I know that I cannot earn my way into heaven and am not worthy of Your favor—it is a free gift of grace. I pray that You will deepen my desire to know You and teach me the principles of Your Word so I can bring honor and glory to Your name. Amen.

JOURNAL QUESTIONS

- If you died today, would you go to heaven? Why?

_____

_____

_____

_____

- What is the means by which people are forgiven?

_____

_____

_____

_____

- How long does salvation last?

_____

_____

_____

_____

- Should people who are saved continue to do good works? Why?

_____

_____

_____

_____

Is it difficult to imagine such an amazing outpouring of grace? Find out
more about God's love for you, the riches of His salvation plan, and
your hope of eternal security at _www.InTouch.org_ today.

PRINCIPLE
3

TRUE EFFECTIVENESS COMES
THROUGH INTIMACY WITH GOD

Before the concept of abiding in Christ became a reality for me, I had already been a pastor for eight years. I'd been to college and seminary, and I thought that the full Christian life meant preaching, studying the Bible, witnessing to people, serving people, and so forth. After eight years, however, I knew there had to be more.

I remember watching a man in my congregation walk down the aisle of our church and rededicate his life to Jesus nearly once a month, sometimes more. Finally I pulled him aside and asked him why he felt the need to continue doing that. He didn't give me a clear reason, but insisted that he needed to rededicate his life. I began to think about the act of rededication and why people do it. I suspect that young man was probably in the same place that I was spiritually—stuck at a dead-end road and trying to make a breakthrough in the only way he could imagine.

At that time, I was preaching on the book of Galatians, and when I came to the fifth chapter, I became genuinely concerned. I thought, *In two more Sundays, I'm going to preach on the fruit of the Spirit, and God will show me that there isn't a lot of peace, love, joy, and goodness in my life.* I remember thinking that I felt a lot more spiritual on Sunday, but Monday through Saturday was a different story.

I knew something was missing. My heart was troubled. I felt inadequate, like a complete failure at the Christian life. I spent hours in our family's camper in our backyard fasting and praying, just trying to get God to do something. In near despair, I prayed, "God, either there is more to the Christian life than I've ever known, or I have to stop telling people who You are. How can I keep preaching if the Christian life is just a set of standards to believe in and there is no real victory? I can't keep going on like this."

As I mentioned earlier, God used the testimony of Hudson Taylor to open my eyes. When I read his testimony, I understood, for the first time in my life, the meaning of JOHN 15:4–5: "Abide in Me, and I in you. As the branch cannot bear fruit of itself unless it abides in the vine, so neither can you unless you abide in Me. I am the vine, you are the branches; he who abides in Me and I in him, he bears much fruit, for apart from Me you can do nothing." Grapes don't just grow; it is the sap running through the vine that brings them to life. I realized that I had been striving to live the perfect Christian life since I was twelve years old but still couldn't do it. I was so overwhelmed I couldn't even pray. I just dropped to my knees. For the first time, I realized that I wasn't supposed to live the Christian life; I was to allow Christ to live it through me. That discovery radically changed my world. It was the major turning point in my whole Christian experience. Since then, my fervent prayer has been that everyone who comes to a saving knowledge of the Lord Jesus Christ will have an intimate relationship with Him.

A PASSION TO KNOW GOD

Do you have a strong, intense, overwhelming desire to know God? Are your thoughts of Him sweeping and grand, or is your relationship with

Him superficial and shallow? Knowing God should be the lifelong pursuit of each believer.

During his ministry the apostle Paul was consumed with an ardent desire to know the person of Jesus Christ. To the Philippian church he wrote,

> Whatever things were gain to me, those things I have counted as loss for the sake of Christ. More than that, I count all things to be loss in view of the surpassing value of knowing Christ Jesus my Lord, for whom I have suffered the loss of all things, and count them but rubbish so that I may gain Christ . . . That I may know Him and the power of His resurrection and the fellowship of His sufferings, being conformed to His death . . . I press on so that I may lay hold of that for which also I was laid hold of by Christ Jesus. (PHIL. 3:7–8, 10, 12)

There is quite a difference between knowing about God and knowing God. Far too many people know about God, but do not really know the person of Jesus Christ. Their relationship with Him—if they have one at all—is very superficial. Knowing Jesus Christ involves a progressively deeper understanding through cultivating an intimate relationship with Him.

Too many Christians are content to know Jesus only as their Savior. They are grateful that their sins are forgiven, that heaven is their destiny. But they are content to rest there, unwilling to pursue the real meaning of eternal life: knowing Jesus (JOHN 17:3).

I have counseled many people who could not find reality with God, however hard they tried. Our churches are full of people who dutifully read their Bibles, pray, and attend church but seem to be on spiritual autopilot. They faithfully go through the motions, yet intimacy with God evades them. I sympathize with the person in this situation, but the truth is, in every case I have seen, that individual failed to surrender something to God.

A fine Christian young man bluntly said to me, "Well, this is as good as I'm gonna be and as far as I'm gonna go." That was the first time I had heard someone come right out and say, "Don't count on me for any more than this. This is as good as I'm gonna be."

Whenever you draw a line between you and the Lord Jesus over any issue, you have chosen failure. By refusing to put something on the altar for Christ, however small it may be, we limit our relationship with Him and shut out the very source of our lives. We often define ourselves much more narrowly than God does, and because of our own feeble selfishness, we miss His best for our lives. If there is anything in your life that means more to you than Christ, you will never know the fullness of His love. Because God loves you, He will discipline you. Ultimately you might yield to Him, or perhaps you will insist on having your way and die without attaining your highest reward in life.

Nothing pleases God more than our full surrender, and He rewards it abundantly. God says, "The one who comes to Me I will certainly not cast out" (JOHN 6:37). It is never God's fault when our relationship with Him wanes. More than anything else our Father in heaven wants an intimate relationship with His children.

Paul was never complacent when it came to knowing Christ. He always hungered and thirsted for more, realizing that God would reveal as much of Himself as Paul desired. He wanted to experience the power of the Lord's resurrection in his daily endeavors, seeing the risen Christ at work in his personal ventures. How dangerous to think we can come to a plateau in our relationship with Jesus Christ! There is no neutral gear in the Christian faith. If we seek to coast, we can be sure we will backslide, not advance, in our personal knowledge of Him.

Knowing Jesus as our Lord radically rearranges our priorities, alters our perspective on adversity and success, and influences our relationships and decision-making processes. Christ becomes the focus and center of our entire lives. We desire above all else the great peace we derive from knowing Him—peace so great that we are willing to suffer loss in everything so that we might come to experience His presence and working in our lives. Our prestige, our possessions, our losses, and our heartaches are but "rubbish" when compared with the blessing of knowing Jesus (PHIL. 3:8). Discovering His faithfulness, experiencing His help, and embracing His purposes bring meaning and significance to every facet of life.

Paul valued the living, experiential knowledge of Jesus Christ as life's highest goal. He was willing to undergo harsh treatment and imprisonment if the adversity would help him to know his Savior more fully. He could tolerate his afflictions because he viewed them in the light of a broader spiritual goal: experiencing and knowing the sufficiency of Christ in every situation.

Have you come to the point where you can agree with Paul's confession of dependence on Christ? Are you willing to regard anything you count valuable as loss if forfeiting it means growing in the grace and knowledge of Christ? Is knowing Christ your ultimate objective?

The prophet Hosea wrote, "Let us know, let us press on to know the LORD. His going forth is as certain as the dawn; and He will come to us like the rain, like the spring rain watering the earth" (HOS. 6:3). God's promises are sure. If we set our hearts and minds to know Him, He will open our spiritual eyes and ears, revealing Himself in wonderful and often unexpected ways. Although the world offers enticing substitutes, nothing can compare to the value of a genuine, growing, passionate relationship with Jesus Christ. We read in COLOSSIANS 2:3 that "all the treasures of wisdom and knowledge" are hidden in Christ. When our foremost passion is to know God, He assures us He will provide for the rest of our needs (MATT. 6:33).

HOW DO WE MAKE KNOWING CHRIST OUR HIGHEST GOAL?

To spend time with the Lord and hear His voice, you must be quiet. Acknowledge that you are seeking something, say, an answer to a pressing need. Then read and meditate on His Word. Inquire of Him and listen for His response. Oftentimes His answer doesn't come when we're praying; it comes when we're not praying. I think sometimes God delays so that we don't get in the habit of sending up "quick fix-it" prayers. By asking Him and listening for His response, we sometimes "hear" through circumstances or other revelations.

I used to lie down on the floor when I prayed. Due to back problems, I can't do that anymore, but I have learned that when I get up early in the morning, the best thing I can do is sit up in bed. I don't get out of bed because I will inevitably become distracted. I just start right then. I ask God to speak to my heart and show me what to do. The more frequently you spend time with the Lord, the more familiar His voice becomes. It's like a cloud clearing from your mind. You know God is speaking. And when you hear His answer, you can face the world. You know with absolute certainty that God has told you what He's going to do. And He always keeps His word.

Throughout all these years, God has never failed me. He has kept every promise that He has made to me. Always. There are some times that I'd like to force a promise from Him, but that doesn't work. When I come to my senses and think about it, I realize that what He wants is best. When you ask for something that's not of God, I think there's always a little check in your spirit that creates a bit of doubt. No matter how sure you think you are, if your petition is not of God, He will not give you total assurance.

Hearing the Scriptures on Sunday morning or through other means is helpful, but there is no substitute for spending time alone with the Savior.

Spiritual intimacy requires quiet moments when God can speak clearly to your heart and when you can speak honestly to Him. We need to spend time alone in prayer, meditation, and worship of Christ. We come to hear from Him, not just receive from Him. We come to adore Him, praise Him, and delight in Him.

We also must give ourselves to the study of the Scriptures. The Bible reveals who God is and what He has done. If we really want to know Him, we will set aside time to partake of the living Word, letting His divine counsel saturate our minds. Reading spiritual biographies of godly people can further augment our walk with God as we observe how He has worked in their lives. They have a great deal to tell us about God's ways.

I encourage you to lay aside any desire in your life that supersedes your passion to know Christ. Jesus wants all of you, not just a part. You can start today. You can begin to know God on a new, deeper level by admitting your need and asking Him to lead you into the knowledge of Him. When knowing God becomes the passion of your life, you, too, can learn to "count all things to be loss in view of the surpassing value of knowing Christ Jesus" (PHIL. 3:8).

KNOWING GOD AS YOUR FATHER

When you pray, by what name do you address God? While all of the grandiose titles we have given Him are appropriate, we Christians have the awesome privilege of calling God "Father." We can also *know* Him that way. I'll never forget the day this reality came to life in me. I was seated in my office when our administrative assistant walked in with her nine-month-old baby. I stood to admire the infant, and before I could offer a word of praise, she thrust the child into my arms. As I looked down at the tiny baby, I realized she was the same age I was when my father died. Whenever people asked me about him, I simply told them that he died when I was too young to know him. But as I stood holding that baby, I realized that *he* had known *me*. Our relationship with God is the same. He tells us, "Before I formed you in the womb I knew you, and before you were born I consecrated you" (JER. 1:5).

The possibility of having a personal relationship with God was a revolutionary concept before Christ lived as a human (MATT. 6:9). The Old Testament contains only fifteen references to God as "Father," and those speak primarily of Him as the Father of the Hebrew people; the idea of Him being a personal God to individuals is not evident until the New Testament. Yet that is the reason Jesus Christ came to earth—to die on the cross for our sins and reveal the heavenly Father so that you and I might know Him intimately.

"Father," which appears 245 times in the New Testament, was Jesus' favorite terminology for God—He spoke it more than ten times just in the Sermon on the Mount (MATT. 5–7), and He also used the name to begin prayer. The Lord's purpose was to reveal that God is not merely a transcendent force somewhere in the universe but a loving, personal, heavenly Father who is profoundly interested in the details of our lives.

Too many people, including believers, do not think of God as being close like a parent, especially if they are living in disobedience. Yet Scripture repeatedly refers to Him as "Father." Paul's letters, for example, begin that way, and the apostle described believers as the household or family of God—he called them God's children and joint heirs with His Son, Jesus Christ (ROM. 8:17).

The privilege of knowing God as Father involves more than acquaintance with Him as a person or Spirit; it goes beyond simple familiarity with His matchless grace, love, and kindness, and even surpasses knowing Him in His holiness, righteousness, and justice. How wonderful that we—mere creations—are able to know Him personally as our very own heavenly Parent. By addressing Him as "Father," Jesus revealed His intention that we understand what the Old Testament saints could not fully grasp:

we can have the blessing of intimate kinship with the living God of the universe.

In fact, it is through the person of Jesus Christ that we are able to know God in this way. Unfortunately many people mistakenly think that such privilege belongs to all humanity. We sometimes hear phrases like "fatherhood of God" and "brotherhood of man"; these official-sounding terms express the faulty idea that God is everybody's Father and we are everybody's brother. Of course, since God is the Creator of life, we could in one sense identify Him as the Father of mankind. But the Bible uses the name "Father" to indicate a close, personal relationship, which certainly is not true of all humanity.

When Jesus gave His disciples a pattern for prayer, He addressed His words to "our Father in heaven" (MATT. 6:9 NKJV). Some people argue that this prayer is for everyone to pray, but notice the very next line: "Hallowed be Your name." Immediately after the reference to our relationship with the heavenly Father is the mention of God's holiness, the very attribute that separates sinful man from Him. So, while it is true that everybody can *pronounce* this prayer, only those who can truly call God their Father have a right to pray it.

Furthermore, Jesus said, "No one comes to the Father but through Me" (JOHN 14:6). An attempt to approach the Father by circumventing the Son is the equivalent of calling Jesus a liar. The key is that the name "Father" implies a relationship and membership in a family. Christ is the door into the family (JOHN 10:9; GAL. 3:26), so how can an unbeliever claim to be a relative while rejecting the one entrance into God's household?

Jesus shed more light on the subject when He told the unbelieving Pharisees, "My word has no place in you. I speak the things which I have seen with *My* Father; therefore you also do the things which you heard from *your* father" (JOHN 8:37–38, emphasis added). From this we know that there are two spiritual fathers in the universe. One of them is Jehovah, the Father of the Lord Jesus Christ. But who is the other? Jesus spelled it out for them: "You are of your father the devil, and you want to do the desires of your father. He was a murderer from the beginning, and does not stand in the truth because there is no truth in him . . . But because I speak the truth, you do not believe Me" (VV. 44–45).

That sounds severe, but since our Savior always speaks truth (JOHN 14:6), His words are trustworthy. Jesus is saying that unless you are by faith related to Jehovah, your spiritual father is Satan. Jehovah is the spiritual Father only to those who love Jesus Christ and trust Him as Savior. Unless you can claim that, you have rejected the Son of God, you have denied His sacrifice on your behalf at Calvary, and as difficult as it may be to accept, the devil is your father.

If you are unsure whose family you are in, take a moment to ask: *Do I use God's name in profanity one minute but then say I believe in Him the next? Do I call upon Him during a crisis but ignore Him at other times? Do I love Jesus?* Remember: the Bible says that if you do not know the Son, you cannot know the Father (JOHN 14:6).

And that is why Jesus Christ came into the world—to give us a glimpse of who the Father is and what He is like. As JOHN 1:18 (NLV) says, "No man has ever seen God. But Christ has made God known to us." Jesus in fact told us, "He who has seen Me has seen the Father" (JOHN 14:9). How did the Son of God reveal His Father? He called the children to Himself and held them in His arms; He healed the sick; He met people's needs. In short, He did all the things a father would do.

HOW GOD EXPRESSES FATHERHOOD

By observing God's fathering pattern, we can better understand our relationship with Him. And by following His lead, we will be able to express parenthood properly to our own children. With that in mind, notice these seven aspects of His Fatherhood to us.

HE DESIRES AN INTIMATE RELATIONSHIP WITH US

The Bible tells us to address Him as "Father," and not just as "God," "King," "Holy One," or "Judge." While we should know Him in all these ways, He wants us to realize we can and should approach Him openly and transparently about everything, including needs, weaknesses, and failures.

GOD LONGS TO COMMUNICATE WITH US

MATTHEW 6:6 tells us to find a secluded place and pray to our Father, "who sees what is done in secret [and] will reward" us. In other words, He hears when we speak to Him, and He answers prayer. He is the kind of Father we can talk to, and though He may not give us everything we want, He will respond to our requests by giving what He knows is best for us (MATT. 7:7–11).

GOD LOVES EACH OF US UNCONDITIONALLY

It is God's nature to love both saint and sinner, based exclusively on the fact that He *is* love (1 JOHN 4:8). The unbeliever has simply positioned himself in such a way that he cannot experience that love—a situation that can be remedied by trusting Jesus as Savior.

OUR HEAVENLY FATHER MEETS ALL OUR NEEDS

Scripture assures us that God knows our needs, even before we ask Him, and He will supply them all "according to His riches in glory in Christ Jesus" (MATT. 6:8; PHIL. 4:19). His resources are limitless, so we can be certain no need will go unmet.

GOD DISCIPLINES HIS CHILDREN (HEB. 12:5–10)

He trains us not out of anger, but with loving correction for our own good. This training is evidence that we are truly His children.

GOD ALWAYS GUIDES US TO DO WHAT IS RIGHT

Jesus said the Holy Spirit—our Counselor—would guide us into all truth (JOHN 14:26; 16:13). God never leads us in the wrong direction; He will make our "paths straight" if we trust Him instead of our own intuition (PROV. 3:5–6).

OUR HEAVENLY FATHER IS ALWAYS WITH US

While human parents cannot guarantee they will *physically* be with their children forever, in another sense, they can always "be there." For example, to this day I can hear the way my mother pronounced "Charles" when she prayed for me and called my name before God. I still recall specific prayer requests she made on my behalf, and I continue to sense her compassion, love, and concern for me. Though I left my house at age eighteen to attend college, I never got away from *home*—I still live with my mother's challenges to be my best and do my best. Even more so, God promises never to leave or forsake us (HEB. 13:5), and His Spirit, which dwells within us, is always available to guide and prompt us.

Do you know God as your heavenly Father? If not, realize that He stands ready to adopt you into His family (ROM. 8:15; GAL. 3:26). All it takes is trusting His Son, Jesus Christ, as your personal Savior. JOHN 1:12 tells us that "as many as received Him, to them He gave the right to become children of God, even to those who believe in His name."

WHY GOD SPEAKS

The God we serve is not a distant, silent deity. He has been communicating with His creation since the beginning (GEN. 2:16), occasionally by an audible voice, but also in other ways (EX. 3:4; HEB. 1:1). Since the first century, He has spoken to us through His Son, Jesus Christ (HEB. 1:2), and He continues to speak as we read Scripture, pray, and seek godly counsel from other believers.

You might wonder, *Why would God want to communicate today? What does He have to say to us?* I believe there are several reasons God speaks. The first is that He loves us and desires an intimate bond with His children. As with any growing relationship, conversation has to flow in two directions: we must be willing not only to talk to Him, but also to listen to Him.

A second reason is to give us guidance. God's people today need as much wisdom and counsel as did the saints of the Bible—we still require direction regarding finances, family, career, church, health, and daily life. Divine wisdom is essential if we are to make sound decisions. This is the reason God sent the Holy Spirit to be our Guide and Teacher (John 16:13; 14:26).

One way the Spirit works is by "illumination"—this happens when we are reading God's Word and suddenly His message to us becomes clear. If we want the Spirit to illuminate the deep truths of the Lord, we've got to give Him something to work with. We must regularly take in words of Scripture so that He can help us understand their meaning.

Another reason for His speaking is to bring us comfort and assurance. In Scripture, God spoke to numerous people undergoing hardships and persecution; reminding them of His sovereign control over their situations fortified their faith. We are no different from the people of Bible times— just as the children of Israel needed God's confidence to cross the Red Sea, you and I go through turbulent experiences in our lives, and our faith also needs to be strengthened.

A final reason—and, I believe, the primary one—is that God wants us to know Him. Though we can never fully grasp all the facets and wonders of who God is, He wants us to spend our lives discovering more and more about Him. He speaks to you, His child, in order to reveal more of His limitless qualities.

OUR FATHER'S VOICE

God uses a number of methods to communicate with us: He speaks through His Word and the Holy Spirit as well as through people and circumstances. God has specific purposes for imparting His thoughts to us. He desires that we comprehend His truth so that it can shape our lives and so that we can share His good news with others.

If God has a particular intention for communicating with us, we have to ask, "What happens when we fail to listen?" We can find the answer at the beginning of the Bible, in the account of Adam and Eve. We know that God spoke very clearly to the first man (GEN. 2:16–17), instructing him not to eat from the Tree of the Knowledge of Good and Evil. The issue is that the first man and woman understood perfectly (GEN. 3:2–3) but did not obey. Their disobedience marks the beginning of man's sin problem, which has plagued the human race throughout history. Every person born thereafter—with the single exception of the Lord Jesus Christ—came into this world with a sinful nature originating from Adam. You and I have never met a perfect person. All sin, suffering, heartache, problems, war, bloodshed, and violence can be traced back to their origin in the Garden.

Unfortunately what occurred in the first family centuries ago has been happening in some form with every family since then. As with Adam and Eve, once we have received God's instructions, we, too, are accountable for what we have heard or read. We can avoid much heartache and trouble by listening to the Lord's communication; failure to listen results in severe repercussions. By studying the account in GENESIS 3, we can identify eight consequences of ignoring the Lord's instructions:

1. WE END UP LISTENING TO THE WRONG VOICES (VV. 1–2)

Eve had unmistakably heard God's command. But even having understood, she began to listen to another voice. The serpent spoke and inserted a question mark into her recollection of God's words: "Indeed, has God said . . . ?" The woman allowed herself to be drawn into conversation with him. The voice she listened to was unfamiliar—it was the voice of neither her Creator nor her husband, yet she paid attention and allowed it to supplant God's clear instruction. As a result, she fell into sin—just like anyone today who stops listening to God and offers an ear to Satan.

Consider how many voices we hear in a given day. What we read and hear continually bombards our minds, hearts, and spirits. Between the television, the radio, the newspaper, and magazines—not to mention the opinions of friends and coworkers—we are barraged with vain, erroneous, ungodly philosophy. We must choose whether or not to listen to it. When we fail to heed God's words or to continually remind ourselves of scriptural principles, we begin to listen to wrong voices, and then we drift away from God.

2. We Are Easily Deceived (Gen. 3:4)

Notice how Satan took what God said and distorted it. The Lord told Adam and Eve that if they ate from the Tree of the Knowledge of Good and Evil, they would "surely die" (Gen. 2:17). Satan used just enough truth to sound credible, but then embellished ever so slightly: "You surely will not die!" It is Satan's nature to lie and deceive, "because there is no truth in him . . . he is a liar and the father of lies" (John 8:44).

Satan deceives with what he knows will appeal, not the truth. He says, "You need this," "You ought to have that," or "This is exactly what you have been looking for." He probably said, "Now, Eve, you need to get the full picture: God doesn't want you to know what He knows, because the day you eat of that tree's fruit, you are going to be just like God." It so happens that Eve did learn some things when she partook. How many of us have learned some things we wish we never knew?

3. We Yield to Pride and Independence (Prov. 16:17–19)

The ultimate root of all sin is pride—it is the equivalent of our saying that we know better than God and can handle the situation our own way.

This is in reality an act of rebellion because it is impossible to know better than an omniscient, all-wise God. His commands are not given to make life dull; every single "thou shalt not" in the Bible is an expression of His love and protection for His children.

4. WE MAKE DECISIONS THAT APPEAL TO THE FLESH (GEN 3:6)

Satan never tempts us by offering spiritual growth, improved prayer life, or more effective ways to share our faith. No, Satan always appeals to the flesh, not to the spirit. There is nothing wrong with God-given desires, but Satan takes our legitimate longings and, with our cooperation, gets them out of balance. As he did with Eve, the devil appeals to three yearnings we all have—human appetites, beauty, and wisdom. Then he twists them so that instead of simply desiring and enjoying them, we begin to lust after them and be controlled by them. So, what God gave in freedom ends up enslaving us. By relying on the Holy Spirit, however, we can have the wisdom and direction to keep yearnings within the parameters God designed for us.

5. WE EXCUSE OUR WRONGS AND BLAME OTHER PEOPLE (GEN. 3:12–13)

When God asked Adam why he was hiding, he immediately pointed at Eve. In fact, there is even a sense of his blaming God for having given him the woman! In turn, Eve blamed the serpent. Neither one could rightly pass the blame because both knew the command and were therefore responsible. Besides, the devil can't make a believer do anything; we may consent to give in to his temptation, but we are ultimately accountable for that decision. People today blame everyone from parents and coworkers to society itself. But we must recognize that passing the buck doesn't solve anything and that we are responsible before God for our choices and behavior.

6. We Suffer the Consequences (Gen. 3:14–19)

All three parties involved had to face the results of their disobedience. Satan was sentenced to eventual destruction. Next, God announced that woman would be ruled by man and would experience pain in childbirth. He also declared that man would have to leave the Garden and toil laboriously to earn a living. Furthermore, humans would ultimately experience death.

At this point, some people look at the penalties and see only harshness. However, what God did amidst His justice—amidst His condemnation of their sin—was to provide a way for them to be forgiven and cleansed. If He did not do something to remedy the situation, mankind would now be eternally and hopelessly separated from Him. So "the LORD God made garments of skin" (GEN. 3:21). In the very first book of the Bible, we see not only the justice of God but also His grace, doing for Adam and Eve what they absolutely could never have done for themselves. They wouldn't have known what to do, nor would they have known how to do it.

If you have never trusted Jesus Christ as your personal Savior, you are just as helpless as Adam and Eve were. The only possible way your sins are going to be forgiven is for you to come to the cross, where Jesus Christ died. The covering of our sin is strictly by the grace of almighty God, and it is symbolized in the shedding of the blood and providing of the skins.

7. We Cause Others Around Us to Suffer (Gen. 3:6, 17–19)

We have seen how sin and its resulting misery extended from the first woman to the first man when she gave him the forbidden fruit. Anguish continued to spread as sin further poisoned their family: the Bible records that Adam and Eve's firstborn son, Cain, murdered his younger brother, Abel. In the earth's very first family, we witness murder, jealousy, and strife. Down through the centuries, Satan has in one way or another had his impact of discord, turmoil, or bloodshed in all families. Everyone is affected because sin is not something that we can isolate. In other words, if you and I sin against God, we are going to hurt somebody else.

8. WE MISS OUT ON GOD'S BEST

When God created Adam and Eve, He intended for them to live in the Garden of Eden with all of its absolute perfection. There, God had provided for their every possible need, and in addition, they felt no guilt or shame (GEN. 2:25). Yet they chose to disobey, and as a result, the first family suffered horrible consequences, including being cast out of their flawless environment.

Although sin has spread to the entire human race, there is good news: you can be forgiven of your sin. But there is only one way, and that is by receiving the Lord Jesus Christ as your personal Savior. Keep God's words and doctrines ever before you—by frequently and regularly spending time in His Word, by participating in corporate worship, by building your knowledge and applying it to your life, principle by principle. If you constantly refresh your heart and mind with God's truth, you will be able to resist the lure of competing voices. When this is difficult, God will move heaven and earth to get your attention—He loves you *that* much!

HIS PRESENCE IS SURE

I've lived alone for the past twelve years. If somebody had told me a decade ago that I could do it, I'd have said, "No way." And yet today I have the most awesome sense of peace and happiness and joy in my heart because I know I'm never really alone. There was a time when walking into my empty home bothered me, but after a while the Lord reminded me that He is always with me. I think of how much more time I have these days to spend with Him. He turned what, at first, was my complaint into a real comfort. I know now that He is adequate and that He will turn the lonely hours into a fruitful time in my life. In fact, He's already done that.

There is no substitute for personal intimacy with God. Nothing compares with it—it is the key to everything. Most people are looking for an exciting and fulfilling life, and they're looking in all the wrong places: money, prestige, and relationships—mostly relationships. They are looking for something that they can achieve to bring about fulfillment, or someone they can meet who will make their small life grow. But there isn't anything we can do or anyone we can meet who will sufficiently fill the void in our hearts. As Thomas Aquinas said, "There is a God-shaped void in all of us." The only thing that can fill the indescribable longing within each human heart is God's presence. The gift of His Son abiding in us is totally adequate for everything we do.

In order to experience intimacy with the heavenly Father, you must genuinely regard Him as more important than everything else you pursue in life. It is important to have goals and relationships, but your primary pursuit should be to know God. When I think about all the things I have been through in my life, I consider my relationship with God absolutely paramount. He has always been there to assure me and bring me through life's trials, however hard they have been.

SUGGESTED BIBLE READING

John 1:18; 6:37; 8:37–45; 14:6–9, 26; 15:4–5;
16:13; 17:3; Philippians 3:7–12; 4:19; Hosea 6:3;
Colossians 2:3; Matthew 5–7; Jeremiah 1:5;
Romans 8:15–17; John 10:9; Galatians 3:26;
1 John 4:8; Hebrews 1:1–2; 12:5–10; 13:5;
Proverbs 3:5–6; Genesis 2:16–17, 25; 3; and
Exodus 3:4.

PRAYER

Dear heavenly Father, I know that I cannot
manufacture a desire to love You as deeply as I ought.
I pray that You will place in my heart a hunger for
Your Word and a longing for fellowship with You.
Amen.

JOURNAL QUESTIONS

- What does it mean to "abide in Christ"?

_____

_____

_____

_____

_____

_____

- Is knowing Christ your ultimate objective?

_____

_____

_____

_____

_____

_____

Does the Christian life not seem to work for you?
Discover the role of the Holy Spirit in shaping and empowering your
walk of faith at *www.InTouch.org* today.

PRINCIPLE
4

TRUST THE LORD, AND HE WILL MOVE HEAVEN AND EARTH TO ACCOMPLISH HIS PURPOSE

CAN YOU TRUST GOD?

When things are going your way, trusting the Lord is easy. But when painful trials come into your life, leaving you frustrated, anxious, or despairing, do you trust Him then? In the face of adversity, many people wonder, *Does God really love me?* and they conclude that a truly caring Father would not allow sorrow and difficulty to touch His children's lives. Oftentimes they start to question whether He is even *willing* to do anything about their circumstances.

God assured His people, "Call upon Me in the day of trouble; I shall rescue you" (Ps. 50:15). Can we truly rely upon Him to do that? Followers of Jesus Christ need to understand that He is not only able but also willing to fulfill every single promise in Scripture. Even when we cannot understand why God would allow certain situations to occur, there are three essential truths that form the basis for trusting Him, no matter what.

THE FIRST TRUTH IS THAT GOD IS PERFECT IN HIS LOVE

In other words, He *always* does what is best for us. If we really believe this, we will trust Him even in our most difficult trials. Satan, who works to undermine our trust, often takes advantage of adversity by calling the Father's motives into question. He whispers, "If the Lord really loved you, He would not have allowed this to happen"—he wants us to associate the sting of spiritual discipline with a lack of divine caring. However, the exact opposite is true. HEBREWS 12:6 tells us, "Those whom the Lord loves He disciplines, and He scourges every son whom He receives." So, while natural thinking says peace and happiness are tokens of God's love, the Bible says difficulty and discipline are actually evidence of our membership in His family. The reason is clear: God cares for us so much that He will not allow us to stay as we are. Instead, He wants to transform us into the likeness of His Son.

We can depend on God's love because of His character—it is His very nature to love (1 JOHN 4:8). The Bible says, "In Him there is no darkness at all" (1 JOHN 1:5); in other words, He is absolutely holy, righteous, and perfect and therefore could never mistreat one of His children. He will always do what is positive and caring in our lives. *Calvary* is positive proof of God's profound love for mankind. All of us were in dire need of forgiveness and rescue from the penalty of sin, but we could not save ourselves—our debt could be satisfied only by the payment of a perfect life (DEUT. 17:1). The heavenly Father made our salvation possible by sending His Son, Jesus, to die on the cross as our substitute, which is indisputable evidence of His sacrificial, infinite love for humanity (ROM. 5:8). God's love is also revealed in the covenant expressing His intention to make us His children (JER. 31:33). Once we trusted Jesus Christ as our personal Savior, we became members of God's family. Our perfect heavenly Father is patient, loving, and kind toward us; He understands that we are children learning to live in this life.

God loves us flawlessly. Every action He performs or permits in our lives is an expression of His love, even though He allows some situations that we think could not possibly be for our good. Always remember that God is omniscient—He sees the end from the beginning and knows exactly what fruit will come from our pain and challenges. Although we may not understand His reason for allowing certain hardships, our difficulties in no way indicate He is anything but a good God.

THE SECOND ESSENTIAL TRUTH IS THAT GOD IS INFINITE IN WISDOM

He never has to poll the angelic host—or anyone else—to get a consensus about the wisest action to take. In His unlimited knowledge, He always knows what is in our very best interest and acts accordingly. Regardless of what our circumstances look like, we must remember that God knows the optimal course of action in every situation and will only benefit His children.

Sometimes we look at difficulties facing us and think, *Well now, Lord, I know You are infinitely wise, but I think You've forgotten something.* Be assured He has not overlooked a single factor. In our limited understanding and reasoning, we simply do not see things from God's perspective. We may have all the information that is humanly possible to gather, but God is aware of *everything* influencing the situation as well as all the potential consequences for you and others. He alone comprehends the totality of every single decision. And because He is infinitely wise, He simply cannot make a mistake (PROV. 3:5–6).

While He completely understands every situation, He is under no obligation whatsoever to inform us of the rationale for His actions or decisions. For example, God did not make clear why He let Joseph languish unjustly in prison for thirteen years before elevating him to the position of prime minister (GEN. 39–41). Nor did He spell out why the Israelites had to live more than four centuries in Egyptian bondage before He miraculously rescued them and made them into a nation (EX. 12:41).

Probably one of the hardest things for me is to see some of the most wonderful, godly people I know stricken with malignant cancer. No matter how much you pray and trust God, they sometimes die. The outcome looks grim, but I can't do anything about it. I feel completely helpless.

In the ministry, I see a lot of sick people. Young and old alike are stricken with diseases that weaken their bodies and disable them. I think of the war veterans I have known; some of them are in wheelchairs unable to walk or even feed themselves. It seems those with physical afflictions have the frailest bodies but the sweetest spirits. I think, *God, I've been physically blessed all of my life, while others have suffered all of theirs.* There are just some things I don't understand—I never boast of understanding. I just have to say, *God, You're in control. You see the end result. If I could see the end result in that person's life, or if I could see what You're doing worldwide, then I'm sure I would agree with You. But at this point I don't know how I can do anything except trust that in Your wisdom, You know what is the best thing to do.*

While we have no right to fully know God's reasons, our lack of such information is the very thing that creates our feelings of frustration, anxiety, and doubt. Consider the irony of the situation. If we in our limited human wisdom *could* comprehend God's motives and actions, that in itself would be cause to doubt Him, since His thinking would be no better than our own! But because God's logic vastly exceeds our own (ISA. 55:8–9), we *can* trust Him—we have no legitimate cause for doubting because He is an infinite, all-wise God who knows the best action to take in our lives.

THE THIRD ESSENTIAL TRUTH IS THAT GOD IS COMPLETELY SOVEREIGN IN HIS CONTROL

He has absolute authority over everything in creation. In other words, if even one tiny event in the universe happened outside God's power and control, we could no longer trust Him—in that case, we couldn't have certainty that He would work every situation for our best interest. But we can trust Him because He *is* sovereign and therefore has perfect, complete control over every last detail of life.

When Pilate asked Jesus, "Do You not know that I have authority to release You, and I have authority to crucify You?" the Lord answered him, "You would have no authority over Me, unless it had been given you from above" (JOHN 19:10–11). Earlier, Jesus reassured His disciples that not even a common sparrow—worth only half a penny—could fall to the ground apart from the Father's will (MATT. 10:29). In other words, whether the circumstance is large or small, God is in absolute control.

Some might ask, "Then what about plane crashes or fires or terrorist attacks? Where is God in all that?" He is still in total control, though this is a perplexing idea for the human mind to reconcile. Some people find comfort in the idea of luck, fate, and chance because trusting God can seem difficult when tragedy strikes. But what happens to God's perfect love, infinite wisdom, and total sovereignty if luck, fate, and chance play a role? These words shouldn't even be in the believer's vocabulary— we would never be able to trust God if events could take place outside His control.

It snowed in Georgia recently—a rare occurrence—and the roads were so icy that most of Atlanta's churches closed their doors. I don't watch television very often, but I found myself alone at home that morning with extra time. I settled in to watch a documentary I'd previously taped about Auschwitz and the Nazis. For almost two hours, I sat in my living room completely overwhelmed by what I saw—every kind of evil imaginable. It was terrible. When the program was over, I walked around my house and thought, *God, how am I to respond to this? This is reality—this kind of evil.* I thought about the vast numbers of people Hitler killed. He, Stalin, and Mao Tse-Tung murdered people thousands at a time. At the hands of those three men, millions of people lost their lives. How am I supposed to respond to such horrors?

I always go back to PSALM 103:19: "The LORD has established His throne in the heavens, and His sovereignty rules over all." I don't know why God allowed the Holocaust to occur. I don't know why thousands of people died at the hands of terrorists on September 11, 2001. Or why a tsunami killed more than 170,000 people in some of the poorest countries on the face of the earth. But I have come to the conclusion that there are some things I'm not going to understand on this side of eternity. Whether its purpose was to awaken the world to the reality of evil or to make us aware of the uncertainty of life, I do not know. I just have to trust God—in some way, in some fashion, He will turn these things to good.

We live in a wicked, vile world where we are subject to the consequences of sin. Many circumstances are not God's perfect will, but He allows them through His permissive will, despite the pain they cause. In His omniscience, God knows what is ultimately best, including the long-term consequences of tragedies that seem heartless and inexplicable. We should not doubt God or abandon our trust when we lack understanding. Instead, we should surrender our lives to Him, accepting by faith that He is good and worthy of our full trust.

Our lives belong to our sovereign, all-knowing, loving God, and nothing can touch us except what He allows. Sometimes that includes hardship and suffering, which leave us wondering, *How can this possibly be good?* And yet many people who have gone through tremendous trials later look back and say, "I hated the difficulty while I was going through it and wondered if God had deserted me. But now, on this side of it, I can see why He allowed it." Not everyone fully understands the spiritual insight, yet it happens frequently enough that we can take comfort, realizing that God has His purposes and with perfect timing will bring blessing from our trials (ROM. 8:28).

So when you face struggles, remind yourself that God has your best interest in mind. He wants you to trust Him as your personal Savior and surrender your life to Him. There is no reason to doubt Him, because He is perfect in His love, infinite in His wisdom, and sovereign in His control of the entire universe. Why should believers ever fret, when even in the deepest, darkest valleys, there can be abiding joy and confidence? No matter what befalls you, our all-loving, all-wise, all-powerful heavenly Father has you in the cradle of His hand.

TRUSTING GOD MEANS LOOKING BEYOND
WHAT WE SEE TO WHAT GOD SEES

The Scripture frequently uses the example of walking as a description of believers' behavior. For example, we are told to walk as children of light, walk in the truth, walk according to the Spirit, and walk in love. COLOSSIANS 2:6 uses this expression to give us an important command: "As you have received Christ Jesus the Lord, so walk in Him." The question we must ask is, "What does it mean to walk in Christ"?

Here, the word *in* does not have a literal usage, like "the hammer is *in* the toolbox." Rather, it refers to a vital relationship—a union between the believer and the Lord. Just as a wedding marks the beginning of a new relationship for a man and a woman, receiving Christ as Savior commences an intimate fellowship between the Lord and His follower. What God desires is not simply to forgive sins, but to develop a close and ever-deepening personal relationship with each of His children. He wants us to realize that the Son of God is the source of everything—Jesus Christ is to the believer what blood is to the body: indispensable to life.

Therefore, "walking in Christ" refers to a dynamic relationship with the Lord. Just as it is impossible to walk while standing still, believers are either moving forward in their Christian life or falling backward. The key for making progress is found in that same Colossians verse: "*As you have received Christ Jesus the Lord*, so walk in Him." How did you and I receive

Christ? By faith. In order to be born again, we trusted the testimony of God's Word. The Christian life is to be "walked"—or lived out—in the same way.

Many people walk by sight and feelings, but allowing our physical senses to guide us spiritually does not work because the Lord simply will not provide all the information we would like to have. Instead, He wants us to trust Him daily for whatever need we may have. That is why followers of Jesus Christ are commanded to "walk by faith, not by sight" (2 COR. 5:7). We must take the first step by faith, and then another, not knowing exactly where it will lead us, but trusting that our omniscient, loving God has our best interest in mind. Walking in faith means having a personal relationship with Jesus Christ that results in trusting Him for every circumstance and believing He will do what is right and what benefits us every time, without exception.

LEARNING TO WALK BY FAITH

What do you do when facing a challenge that seems insurmountable? PROVERBS 3:5–6 instructs you to "trust in the LORD with all your heart and do not lean on your own understanding. In all your ways acknowledge Him, and He will make your paths straight."

The foundation for living a life of faith is a personal relationship with Jesus Christ. Unless we know Him, we cannot discern His will for our lives. When an opportunity unfolds, those who desire to live by faith want to know that it is God who is leading them and not their own motivation.

God has a purpose for every situation we encounter. There are no coincidences with Him. He is the Architect behind every blessing that comes our way. In times of trial and sorrow, He is working in ways unknown to us to bring goodness and hope out of each difficulty. Yet many people wonder if God truly has a plan for their lives. The answer is yes. The first step in understanding this plan comes when we begin to build an intimate relationship with Him. Salvation is the starting point. When we acknowledge our need for a Savior, pray and ask Him to forgive our sins and to cleanse us from all unrighteousness, God rescues us from an eternal death.

God graciously embraces us with His eternal love and mercy. He forgives and washes away the stain that sin has left on our lives (ISA. 1:18). Then He prepares us for blessing—not necessarily in a material sense, but spiritually and emotionally. A person may have tremendous material wealth but be spiritually and emotionally bankrupt. Abraham was not a poor man. He was a leader among his people. God had given him the ability to see beyond the immediate challenge to the blessings of the future.

When God commanded him to sacrifice his only son on the altar, Abraham did not cower in fear or lay awake at night wondering how the Lord would provide for him. He trusted God, and in doing so, he was able to have fellowship with Him. Scripture tells us that Abraham believed God, and his belief was "reckoned" to him as "righteousness" (GEN. 15:6).

There are two things that are essential to living a faith-motivated life. First, we must believe that God exists. Second, we must believe that He does what He has promised to do. HEBREWS 11:6 tells us that "without faith it is impossible to please [God], for he who comes to God must believe that He is and that He is a rewarder of those who seek Him." Faith is not a goal that we must work to achieve. It comes as the overflow of a personal relationship with God. It is as natural as taking a breath of air. Faith is the breath and life of our relationship with God and His Son.

There also are material benefits to abiding by faith. God rewards our desire to trust Him and live obediently. No matter how small our faith seems at times, God is pleased when we depend upon Him. Even the slightest step of faith does not go unnoticed by Him. We can be sure that just as He was faithful to the promise He made to Abraham, He will be faithful to us. One of the greatest blessings Abraham received was being called the friend of God (ISA. 41:8).

Do you trust God with your life? He created you and knows you completely. He understands your weaknesses and your desire to love Him. Even when you feel as though you have failed Him, He is quick to receive you and prove His love to you.

After the Crucifixion, the disciples returned to their former ways of life. Instead of living by faith and doing what God had called them to do, they went back out on the Sea of Galilee to fish (MATT. 4:18; JOHN 21:3–4)! Have you ever wondered how God views our lack of faith? It is certain that He will never condemn us (ROM. 8:1). Christ's presence on the shore of Galilee was enough to let Peter and the others know that it was time to stop being distracted by the voices of the world. Before the Crucifixion, He had told the disciples that He would return to them, and He fulfilled His promise. God has kept every promise He made. This is why we can trust Him with every aspect of our lives.

Although Peter denied knowing Christ, Jesus did not deny knowing him. We may falter and fail, but God does not want us to focus on our shortcomings. Instead, He wants us to set our focus on Him. God evaluates our lives not according to *our* ability to remain faithful, but according to *His* faithfulness and the work that was accomplished at Calvary. While He does not want us to yield to temptation, He knows there will be times when we fall. But always we remain the beneficiaries of His endless grace and eternal love. After the Resurrection, one of the first things Jesus did was to go to Peter and reassure him of His eternal love. God's plan for Peter's life had not changed. Therefore, Jesus encouraged His disciple not to give up. A person who lives by faith will recognize the fact that God never gives up on him.

What does it take to live a life of faith?

A DESIRE TO KNOW GOD AND TO BE KNOWN BY HIM

God desires to know each of His children intimately. Therefore, if you pray for the desire to know Him, you can be certain that He will fill your heart with longing for Him. A genuine desire for God cannot be manufactured, but it can be easily acquired—all you have to do is ask for it.

A Commitment to Obey Him

Obedience is a mark of our ability to trust God, especially when it comes to facing important decisions or serious challenges. God may direct us along a certain course, but we sometimes find ourselves doubting His ability to protect and deliver us safely. However, a person who lives by faith will continue moving forward as Abraham did, without yielding to feelings of doubt or fear. God always rewards obedience with great blessing.

A Confident Conviction that God Will Fulfill Every Promise

The ultimate question is not "Will God do what He promised?" but "Am I willing to trust Him even though His timetable may not be mine?" We must realize that the faith demonstrated by Abel, Enoch, Noah, Abraham, Jacob, and Sarah was faith without limits (HEB. 11). Each one of those people trusted God despite the fact that they did not see the end result of their confidence in Him. They lived by faith each day, and God gave them an eternal reward.

A Lifestyle of Faith

A life of faith is dominated by Jesus Christ, not selfish desires. The person of little faith says, "God can." The person of great faith says, "God will." But the person with perfect faith says, "God has done it."

Are you willing to trust God and see what He will do in your life? God led Abraham into a land of tremendous promise and blessing. He will do the same for you as you trust Him and walk by faith.

BARRIERS TO FAITH

Moses was chosen for a task that he did not believe he could do. Even though God proved Himself to Moses and spoke directly to him through a burning bush, the future leader did not fully trust the Lord to enable him to fulfill that calling. When God chose him to deliver the nation of Israel, Moses retorted, "What if they will not believe me or listen to what I say? For they may say, 'The LORD has not appeared to you'" (EX. 4:1). Although the reluctant servant recounted his many weaknesses, the Lord nevertheless remained firm in His call.

Why do we experience barriers to our faith? Like Moses, many people have a limited understanding of God. At first, he could not comprehend what God was telling him to do. How could he lead millions out of Egyptian bondage? Afraid that he could not rise to the task to which God called him, he presented five reasons to prove his calculations were correct. Perhaps, at some point, you have felt the same way.

1. A POOR SELF-IMAGE

Moses was a shepherd, and Egyptians loathed shepherds. Because he had assessed his life apart from the miraculous work of God, the prophet denied he could be of any use to God. Oswald Chambers wrote, "Don't plan without God. God seems to have a delightful way of upsetting the plans we have made, when we have not taken Him into account."[1] God takes great joy in doing the impossible through the lives of men and women who place their trust in Him. Remember, what seems impossible for you is an opportunity for God to display His infinite ability.

2. IGNORANCE OF WHO GOD IS

Moses had heard the name Yahweh, but he did not have a personal knowledge of the God of Israel. However, this changed when he stepped into the presence of the living Lord at the burning bush. That was where

God began to develop Moses' spiritual character, a process that continued throughout his life.

If you want to grow spiritually while gaining God's wisdom and discernment, begin spending time alone with the Lord on a regular basis. In times of worship, praise, and prayer, God will reveal His loving nature to you.

3. DOUBT

Moses doubted God's ability, and his doubt kept him from experiencing the fullness of His immediate blessings. Each of us has faced times when we were not sure of God's involvement in our circumstances. We have wondered if we could trust His promises, and we have questioned the Christian principles that we had been applying to our lives.

Years ago, when we first moved to Atlanta, my wife and I searched three months for a house and found nothing. Finally, a house became available. It wasn't what we wanted, but we were desperate. I knew God was telling us to wait, but we were living with another couple and their two children, and I didn't feel that we could impose on them any longer. So I put an offer on the house and signed a contract. The very next day my wife found a beautiful Dutch colonial that was absolutely perfect. Our hearts sank as I realized the results of my lack of trust.

Thankfully, God is incredibly gracious—that isn't the end of the story. In the contract I had signed, there was a stipulation stating that if there was any water damage in the basement, it would invalidate the sale. The night we signed our contract, a thunderstorm poured down on Atlanta leaving a foot of water in the house. Our realtor called to say that he couldn't remember the last time he had seen so much rain. The contract was nullified and we purchased the other home—the one God had intended for us to have.

God never allows us to face a challenge without providing a promise for us to cling to in times of trial and adversity. A lack of trust in God's ability often leads to feelings of unrest and anxiety. Doubt keeps us from accomplishing God's will, but it also prevents us from experiencing His goodness.

Moses did not realize it, but the moment he decided to obey God was the first step he took toward an eternal blessing. How do you experience God's goodness? Lay aside your doubts. Place your trust in the omnipotent potential of an all-knowing God who loves and understands you completely and will never allow you to experience defeat.

4. INADEQUACY

One of Moses' strongest excuses was that he could not speak eloquently. Therefore, he argued, he could not go to the people of Israel with God's message, nor could he go to Pharaoh (Ex. 4:10).

A person who thinks he is of great value to God is deceived. Those who know they need God are the ones most often used by Him to do great work. When we think we are bright, talented, and strong, we usually have little need of God. Our minds are set on what we can accomplish, and we do not seek the wisdom of the Lord. But depending solely on our own strength can lead to feelings of doubt, insecurity, and anxiety.

The person with a humble heart knows that he can do nothing apart from God, and this is his greatest asset. Moses was overwhelmed by his challenge, but God's ability surpassed anything he faced. Whatever your inadequacy, it is an opportunity for God to prove His faithfulness through you.

5. FEAR OF FAILURE

Fear of failure is one of the most debilitating and common fears people suffer from. I have counseled countless people who could not move ahead in their careers, relationships, or personal goals because they were afraid of failure. Unable to trust in God's strength, they looked inside at their own human frailty and concluded there was no hope.

Many people are actually more afraid to fail than to die. I am convinced that this is why so many people struggle to rest completely in God's grace—they are afraid He will let them fail. But God will never give you a directive and then leave you to work out the details by yourself. Instead, He is personally involved in every aspect of your life. As believers, we have access to the wisdom and strength of almighty God. When we renounce any feelings of pride, doubt, or fear, God works in our lives to do "abundantly beyond all that we ask or think" (EPH. 3:20).

ACQUIRING GIANT FAITH

We all know the story of the young shepherd boy who slew the giant. David stood before his formidable foe with no sword, no armor, and no battle experience. Biblical commentaries speculate that Goliath, a mammoth warrior, stood somewhere between nine and twelve feet tall and that he weighed several hundred pounds. He was heavily armed, and the sight of him struck terror in the hearts of Saul's army. By all rational accounts, David was no match for his challenger.

At some point, each of us will face what seem to be mammoth trials and difficulties. Knowing how to respond properly to these challenges is critical to our spiritual growth.

The secret of David's success was his ability to trust and obey God. He also realized that faith was progressive: what he learned in one situation, God later applied and reapplied to his life. He wrote, "[God] trains my hands for battle, so that my arms can bend a bow of bronze" (2 SAM. 22:35).

God has a plan to develop our faith. He takes our limited trust and grows it into a strong and mighty faith—one that has the ability to conquer deadly foes. This is often why He allows us to face adversity and challenges of all kinds, good and bad. In times of extreme pressure, God stretches our faith and deepens our dependence on Him. Without strong, abiding trust, we will quickly yield to temptation and fear, especially when the trial or difficulty is intense or prolonged.

God developed David's trust until it became unshakable, and He wants to do this in our lives as well. Whether it relates to the beginning of a new job or the ending of an old one, God wants to teach us to trust Him at every turn in life. Had the nation of Israel learned this, it never would have suffered Goliath's verbal abuse for forty days. The Bible tells us that was how long the Philistine taunted Israel. Both armies mistakenly believed that Goliath was the ultimate offensive weapon, but they had forgotten God (1 SAM. 17).

When David arrived at the battlefront, he could not believe what he was hearing from the mouth of the Philistine giant. Immediately he saw past the physical evidence around him to the spiritual nature of the battle: it was not a battle between men; it was a battle between God and the enemy of our souls—Satan.

One of Satan's primary attacks in the life of a believer is discouragement. Even Jesus warned us not to be concerned about the one who could kill our bodies but, instead, to be aware of the one who could kill our souls. Once we have accepted Christ as our Savior, the enemy assumes a different role. He goes to work on our emotions by trying to persuade us to believe that we are not worthy of God's love and affection. He seeks ways to cause us to feel defeated and discouraged with the goal that if he can make us give up, then we will abandon our commitment and love for God.

However, Satan cannot defeat the love of God. God's love for us is paramount and eternal. He loves us not because of what we do, but because of what His Son did for us on Calvary's cross. There is nothing we can do to become worthy of God's unconditional love. It is simply there for the taking, whenever we are ready to accept it and ask Him to show us how to appropriate it in our lives.

David discovered that God's greatest enemy already had worked his lies into the minds and lives of Israel's soldiers. The soldiers wouldn't go into battle with Goliath because they believed they could not win. Not one arrow had been shot, yet Israel was ready to concede defeat (1 SAM. 17:24). Imagine what they thought when David came on the scene, declaring that God would grant him the victory.

The Goliath in your life may come in the form of financial indebtedness, the death of a loved one, a teenager who has left home, news of a serious illness, a broken relationship, or the betrayal of a friend. God does not want us to sink into feelings of doubt and worry. He is our ever-present help, our rock, our fortress, our deliverer, our refuge, our strength, and our infinite stronghold (PS. 18).

THE FAITH THAT CONQUERS

Whatever Goliath you face, the one truth you need to bury deep within your heart is this: God loves you, and when you place your trust in Him, He will not allow you to face defeat. You may go through times of failure. Life may not always turn out the way you planned, but ultimately God will be glorified, and you will be blessed.

Every challenge presents an opportunity for God to display His faithfulness and love. Instead of yielding to thoughts of fear and failure, make a commitment to trust God, even when you do not know what the next day will bring: "In all your ways acknowledge Him, and He will make your paths straight" (PROV. 3:6).

David's faith was not based on human understanding. It was founded in the sovereignty of God. Therefore, David knew he could not fail in his quest to defeat the Philistine giant.

How do you gain a conquering faith?

RECALL PAST VICTORIES

David recalled how God had delivered him from the paw of the lion and the grasp of the bear (1 SAM. 17:32–37). Spiritual victories are won in your mind. If you give in to feelings of fear, doubt, and unbelief, you will suffer defeat because your mental focus shifts from God and His infinite ability to the lies of the enemy. Set the focus of your heart, mind, and will on the truth of God's Word, and you will gain the victory in every battle.

REEXAMINE AND REAFFIRM YOUR MOTIVES

David did not rush into battle without assessing the situation. He realized that the battle facing Israel was spiritual in nature and not just physical. His primary motivation for seeking the victory was not personal gain. Instead it was to bring glory to God.

If your motives for victory are selfish in nature, God will deal with you. True victory and peace can come only as you surrender your life, along with your desires, to Christ. In yielding yourself to Him, you gain a deeper joy and sense of fulfillment. Always ask three questions before dealing with any conflict or challenge: *What is my motivation? What is God's purpose for me?* and *What really is going on here?* Take time to pray and seek God's will for every situation.

REJECT DISCOURAGING WORDS

There was no one to encourage David in his quest to defeat Goliath. The soldiers laughed at him. His brothers were embarrassed by his presence and urged him to go home. Even King Saul doubted David's ability. If he had listened to their comments, he would have given up. Instead, David turned his heart toward God, and it was there that he found the encouragement he needed. From a human perspective, there may be times when you feel as though you are facing a Goliath alone. But God has promised never to leave you (HEB. 13:5). His Spirit is with you in every circumstance.

RECOGNIZE THE TRUE NATURE OF THE BATTLE

Goliath cursed David when he saw him: "Am I a dog, that you come to me with sticks? . . . Come to me, and I will give your flesh to the birds of the sky and the beasts of the field" (1 SAM. 17:43–44).

David countered these threats with a wonderful reply:

> You come to me with a sword, a spear, and a javelin, but I come to you in the name of the LORD of hosts, the God of the armies of Israel, whom you have taunted. This day the LORD will deliver you up into my hands . . . that all the earth may know that there is a God in Israel, and that all this assembly may know that the LORD does not deliver by sword or by spear; for the battle is the LORD's and He will give you into our hands. (vv. 45–47)

What a victorious answer to the enemy's threat!

RESPOND TO THE CHALLENGE WITH A POSITIVE CONFESSION

David made positive confessions of faith to those around him. He asked his critics, "Who is this uncircumcised Philistine, that he should taunt the armies of the living God?" (1 SAM. 17:26). To Saul he said, "The LORD who delivered me . . . will deliver me from the hand of this Philistine" (1 SAM. 17:37). And to Goliath he said, "I come to you in the name of the LORD of hosts, the God of the armies of Israel" (1 SAM. 17:45). David's words were a testimony of faith. He was convinced that he could not lose, because God was with him.

RELY ON THE POWER OF GOD FOR THE VICTORY

David did not need a spear or a javelin to defeat Goliath. He needed only a conquering faith and a willingness to follow God. A homemade slingshot was the weapon God chose for him. Human strength was not the victor. God was the One who received the glory.

RECKON THE VICTORY

Once you have spent time with God in prayer and know that it is His will for you to enter the battle, you can reckon the victory to be

His. Even before he stepped on the battlefield, David knew he would not lose.

You can face any circumstance with confidence and hope because it is not your strength, wisdom, energy, or power that is the ultimate source of victory. It is God's ability, and when you place your trust in Him, you tap into an eternal force that cannot be harnessed by any human constraints.

SUGGESTED BIBLE READING

PSALMS 18; 50:15; 103:19; HEBREWS 11:6; 12:6;
DEUTERONOMY 17:1; 1 JOHN 1:5; 4:8; ROMANS 5:8;
8:1, 28; JEREMIAH 31:33; PROVERBS 3:5–6; GENESIS
39–41; EXODUS 12:41; ISAIAH 41:8; 55:8–9; JOHN
19:10–11; 21:3–4; MATTHEW 10:29; 14:9;
COLOSSIANS 2:6; 2 CORINTHIANS 5:7; EXODUS
4:1–10; EPHESIANS 3:20; 1 SAMUEL 17; and
2 SAMUEL 22:35.

PRAYER

Dear heavenly Father, thank You for caring about me
enough to send Your Son to atone for my sin. Thank
You for knowing when I get up and when I sleep.
Thank You for the plan You have for my life. I pray
You will help me to trust in You and take my strength
from You to slay the giants in my life. Amen.

JOURNAL QUESTIONS

- Are you able to trust God?

_____

_____

_____

- What are the barriers to your faith?

_____

_____

_____

_____

- Is there a "Goliath" in your life?

_____

_____

_____

- How has God shown Himself faithful to you?

_____

_____

_____

_____

Have you faced obstacles that have caused you to doubt God's love or
power in your life? Visit _www.InTouch.org_ today for
in-depth study of His overarching plan for bringing you
into a new level of spiritual maturity.

PRINCIPLE
5

OBEDIENCE ALWAYS
BRINGS BLESSING

I once photographed a beautiful vineyard in northern California. I was struck by the uniformity of the rows—I had never seen anything in nature as straight. I knelt down to see if I could detect any crooked vines, but I couldn't. They were absolutely perfect. Looking out across those acres of meticulous crops, I thought of how precise God's ways are and how He has given us a simple way to walk the straight and narrow path.

When we obey God, we will experience His blessing; when we don't, we will miss out on that blessing. One of the most basic yet important principles a Christian can ever learn is that of obedience.

The more familiar we become with God's Word, the more we will begin to understand obedience. God's laws are not designed to deprive us of pleasure or prosperity; rather, they are intended to protect us from hurting ourselves and others, and to guide us toward the fulfillment in life that He wants us to enjoy.

When we are faced with daily pressures, we may be tempted to compromise Scripture's express teaching in favor of self-reliance or worldly solutions. Every person has God-given desires and appetites, which can be satisfied as He intended or in selfish and even harmful ways. Throughout our lives, we will encounter opposition to biblical living. Obedience to God involves a commitment to Him, regardless of the consequences.

Obeying God often involves choices that we fear could result in rejection, loss, or hardship. Sometimes the decision to follow Christ brings about unwanted confrontation. Obedience always requires courage. However difficult our circumstances may be, we can respond to them with confidence in the One who empowers us to do His will. Has God ever made a mistake, been too late, or proven inadequate? No! Our heavenly Father is all-powerful and consistently faithful.

The laws of Scripture are profound yet simple: the Bible teaches that we will reap what we sow, more than we sow, later than we sow. When we obey God, we will always get His best; when we don't, life will turn out to be much harder. We do not always do what we should, and there is grace in those situations, but for Christians, making a commitment to obey God is essential to our faith. Obedience and faith are inseparable. We demonstrate our trust in God by complying with His will. When we do so, we will reap the rewards He has designed for us—and we will hit our target every time.

THE KEY TO GOD'S HEART

I was only in the first grade, but I still remember the key that unlocked the door to our house. It was one of those long black keys, and after I left in the morning, I would hide it under a rock so nobody but my mother and I knew where it was. Sometimes I came home in the afternoon and wondered if the key was still there. When I moved the rock aside and spotted it, a wonderful sense of relief flooded over me. The key was important to me because it was the key to our home. It unlocked the place where my mother and I lived—where my needs were met and where our belongings were kept. Home was where I felt my mother's love and care.

More than likely, you also have keys in your life—keys to your house, your car, or your desk. But have you ever thought about having the key to someone's heart? When you have the key to somebody's heart, you know how to reach what is inside. You know how to move that person toward you, and you understand how he or she feels.

For some people, the key may be love, faith, or service. I want to tell you that the key to God's heart is *obedience*. Nevertheless, too many people fail to realize this. Because we're taught to be independent and self-reliant, the idea of obedience doesn't sit well with most people. But God does not fashion Himself according to our vanity. Though it can be difficult and sometimes painful, obedience is what God asks of us. Obedience should be a priority for anyone who desires to know God and please Him. It is always the right choice, with no exceptions. Jesus said, "If anyone loves me, he will obey my teaching. My Father will love him, and we will come to him and make our home with him" (JOHN 14:23 NIV).

SAYING YES TO GOD

God's simple requests are often stepping-stones to life's greatest blessings. Simon Peter is a good illustration of what happens when we say yes to God. In LUKE 5:1–11, people were pressing in around Jesus while He was preaching. The Lord wanted to use Peter's boat as a floating platform from which to address the throng on shore, so He asked the future apostle to push the vessel out a little way (v. 3). That in itself was not a particularly remarkable request, but Peter's compliance paved the way for multiple blessings, and from his example, we learn how essential it is to obey God in even the smallest matters.

Immediately the people were blessed by Peter's obedience—they could hear Jesus' words as He taught. Then, when the lesson was completed, the

Lord said to Peter, "Put out into the deep water and let down your nets for a catch" (v. 4). Here was another opportunity to say yes or no, and Peter must have felt tempted not to consent. After all, he had worked the entire night in hopes of a catch but had returned empty-handed and exhausted. And Jesus was telling him to go fishing! But notice what happened as a result of Peter's obedience: on a day that he and his colleagues had written off as a total loss, they pulled in not one, but two overflowing boatloads of fish (v. 7). Saying yes resulted in a miracle that absolutely transformed the fisherman's life.

Obedience is critical to the successful Christian life, and there are several truths that will help you understand it from a divine perspective:

1. OBEYING GOD IN SMALL MATTERS IS AN ESSENTIAL STEP TO GOD'S GREATEST BLESSINGS

Suppose Peter had said, "I'm busy cleaning my nets right now. I can't help You because I'm going fishing again tonight—I just don't have the time." Or he could have said, "Why don't You ask to use that other boat over there?" or "I've already been fishing today. It would be a waste of time to go again right now." Peter could have said a number of things. If he had said anything other than yes, he would have missed the greatest fishing experience of his life. But because of Peter's obedience, the Lord arranged a miracle that he would never forget.

Oftentimes God's greatest blessings come as a result of our willingness to do something that appeared to be very insignificant. So ask yourself, *Has God been challenging me to do something seemingly unimportant that I have not yet made an effort to accomplish? Is there anything I have rationalized by saying, "It's too difficult," "I don't want to," or even "I have to pray about it"?*

2. OUR OBEDIENCE IS ALWAYS BENEFICIAL TO OTHERS

Think of all the people who were blessed by Peter's obedience. In addition to the crowd being able to see the Lord and hear His lesson, Jesus

Himself benefited: preaching from the boat afforded Him the comfort of being able to sit down while He spoke (v. 3). Not only that, but Peter's friends had a very profitable day—they took in two vessels so full of fish that both began to sink. More important, they had the opportunity to witness something supernatural.

God often rewards other people—especially those closest to us—as a result of our obedience. For example, no father can be obedient to God without blessing pouring out into the lives of his wife and his children. And a child's obedience will likewise bless his or her parents.

3. Obeying God May Require Doing Some Things That Appear to Be Unreasonable

Peter was a skillful fisherman who knew all the best fishing spots and understood the optimal times and conditions for a catch. Then Jesus, an itinerant preacher and carpenter, approached the seasoned seaman and said, "Let's go fishing." Peter must have been thinking, *He is certainly a wonderful teacher, but I'm the fisherman. We fished all night long with no success, and besides, it is now midday, the worst possible time to net anything.* To his credit, Peter chose to obey (v. 5) and, as a result, experienced a stunning display of divine power.

Our obedience to God should never be based on whether something seems rational or fits with the world's way of thinking. That is not to say God always bypasses common sense, but oftentimes what He requires of us may not appear reasonable or match our preconceived ideas. That was exactly what happened just before I moved to Atlanta. I always believed that to be effective, a pastor needed to stay in one pulpit for a long time. Yet after only eleven months in Bartow, Florida, I began to hear God speak to me about coming to Georgia, which struck me as extremely unreasonable. I gave the Lord reason after reason why I should remain, including that my preacher friends would think I had failed in that position. God was not at all persuaded and kept pressing my heart to do as

He instructed. If I had not submitted—if I had said, "No, God, it is simply not logical"—I would have missed tremendous blessings.

4. WHEN WE OBEY GOD, WE WILL NEVER BE DISAPPOINTED

Because of his experience at fishing, Peter undoubtedly assumed Jesus' instructions would amount to killing time, waiting for nothing to happen. But when he complied with that simple request, he was gripped with amazement at what the Lord brought about. We, like Peter, must recognize that obeying God is always the wise course of action. Jesus turned an empty boat into a full one. He can also take our emptiness—whether it is related to finance, relationship, or career—and change it into something splendid and thriving.

Perhaps you are hesitant to obey because you fear the consequences. Remember that the same sovereign, omnipotent God who keeps your heart beating and the planets orbiting is more than able to handle the circumstances of your obedience. I am not saying that to obey necessarily results in the exact outcome you desire; in fact, an intervening trial could possibly precede a blessing. But even when our expectations do not line up with God's purposes, that in no way means His ways will be disappointing; on the contrary, however He chooses to bless our obedience will ultimately prove far more satisfying.

5. OUR OBEDIENCE ALLOWS GOD TO DEMONSTRATE HIS POWER IN OUR LIVES

If Peter had said no, he would have missed an awesome demonstration of divine power that made his faith skyrocket and marked the beginning of the most thrilling three years imaginable. Walking with the Lord Jesus Christ every day, the disciple would witness miracles even greater than two boatloads of fish—a blind man would begin to see, dead Lazarus would be restored to life, and at Jesus' urging, Peter himself would step out of a boat not into the water, but *onto* it! Why do you think he had the courage to leave his vessel and walk on the water toward Christ? The reason is that Peter started by saying yes to a small request. Then each time God rewarded his obedience, the apostle's faith grew, to the point that he believed his Master not only controlled the fish in the water but also had absolute authority over the water!

6. OBEYING GOD ALWAYS RESULTS IN DEEPER UNDERSTANDING

Prior to this incident, Peter might have been aware that Jesus was a carpenter. He certainly knew Him as a rabbi and had heard the profound truths the Lord taught the crowds. However, obeying Christ's request set the stage for Peter to get brand-new insight—the Lord's holiness and sovereign authority over nature were clearly evident through the miraculous catch. By contrast, the fisherman likely recognized his own sinfulness. When we obey God, we, too, will discover that something happens in our hearts.

7. OBEYING GOD WILL RESULT IN DRAMATIC CHANGES IN OUR LIVES

Simon Peter had in all likelihood intended to spend the rest of his life fishing. But everything changed with one simple act of obedience. He willingly laid down his net and walked into a whole new lifestyle of following the Lord Jesus Christ.

God can revolutionize our lives. For some people, this could mean a change of career, a new location, or a different relationship. Are you willing to do what God says, when and how He says to do it? Are you willing to leave all the consequences to Him? The hymn writer expressed it simply: "Trust and obey, for there's no other way to be happy in Jesus, but to trust and obey." Let me add a truth to that: there is no such thing as happiness apart from Jesus. Without a right relationship with Christ, you will never have real contentment, peace, or assurance. Nothing else in this world can ever truly satisfy.

To become wholly surrendered disciples of Christ, we must begin by obeying Him in every aspect of our lives, however small it may seem. Remember the good servant, who heard his master say, "Well done, good slave, because you have been faithful in a very little thing, you are to be in authority over ten cities" (LUKE 19:17). Unless you say yes to a little request from the Lord, you will never know what your life could have been like—or what wonderful blessing would have been yours if only you had obeyed God. Why risk losing when you can be certain of winning?

THE PRIORITY OF OBEDIENCE

Perhaps you know someone who believes that living a good and honest life gains God's favor. Many people think they are demonstrating obedience to God by helping others occasionally, avoiding temptation, and attending church. But there is much more to obedience. True obedience to God means doing *what* He says, *when* He says, *how* He says, *as long as* He says, *until* what He says is accomplished.

Unfortunately this concept is often rejected in today's culture. We have rationalized disobedience to the point of missing the best of God's blessings. Do you wonder why God doesn't answer your prayers with a yes or why, though you try and try, the circumstances in your life still don't work out? The answer could lie in your level of obedience to God. If you have accepted Jesus Christ as your Savior and yet are still experiencing great spiritual frustration, there may be an area of disobedience in your life that you have not addressed. Perhaps God has asked something of you, and in response, you have ignored His words or done only part of what He requires.

Before you try to make a list of everything God has ever asked you to do or not to do, consider this: Is there *one particular* area of your life in which you struggle to be obedient to God's Word? As you read the Scriptures, does He continually bring a particular sin to your attention?

When you go to Him in prayer, does the same issue surface repeatedly? If the Lord is bringing something to your mind right now, it could be that you have been living in the same situation for years because at some point, you chose to do things *your* way instead of *God's* way.

Understanding this key distinction between our way and God's way can make a tremendous difference in every believer's life. We must place obedience at the top of our priority list. But to do so, we need to fully understand why obedience plays such an important role in our relationship with God. To illustrate this point, I want to discuss people in the Bible who approached obedience in very different ways.

DISOBEDIENCE: ADAM AND EVE

Disobedience always brings about painful consequences. Sometimes those consequences affect only the individual who sins, and sometimes they affect others. Perhaps the clearest illustration of this truth comes from the story of Adam and Eve.

God created a perfect environment for this young couple and gave them just two commands: "Be fruitful and multiply" (GEN. 1:28), and "From the tree of the knowledge of good and evil you shall not eat" (GEN. 2:17). We know that Adam and his wife understood these simple instructions because Eve was able to repeat them to the tempter prior to succumbing to his evil plan (GEN. 3:3). You may be thinking, *Well, things are different today. There are no talking snakes, and we have many instructions on how to live our lives.* That is true, but one thing has not changed. God has offered a path of obedience to each of us, and we have the choice of following it or walking our own way.

Disobedience is rebellion against God—irreverence toward Him. It is a statement from your heart proclaiming that you have chosen your way over God's way. When you are disobedient, you are essentially refusing to acknowledge God's authority, right, and power in your life. In contrast, to avoid disobedience, you must bring your thoughts, actions, words, and goals in line with God's perfect will (2 COR. 10:5). More important, when He gives you words of direction, wisdom, or warning, you must heed them completely.

PARTIAL OBEDIENCE: KING SAUL

Contrary to the belief of some people, perfect obedience does not mean that we have to be perfect people. Obeying God, however, does require *exact* obedience. Let's consider a person who demonstrates what can happen when we do not obey God completely. When we turn to 1 SAMUEL 10, we can follow the case of King Saul and his struggle with total obedience.

Saul received God's instructions to go to Gilgal and wait seven days for the prophet Samuel to join him. The two would then make a burnt offering together (1 SAM. 10:8). Saul started well, but as the seventh day approached, he became restless and frustrated, and finally decided to make an offering without Samuel. But the Bible tells us that "as soon as he finished offering the burnt offering . . . Samuel came" (1 SAM. 13:10). Saul waited *almost* long enough, but partial obedience is not obedience.

We can read the result of this story in verses 13–14: "Samuel said to Saul, 'You have acted foolishly; you have not kept the commandment of the LORD your God, which He commanded you, for now the LORD would have established your kingdom over Israel forever. But now your kingdom shall not endure.'" God does not promise that we will be able to see or understand how His plan for our lives is to unfold. Instead, He often calls us to obey Him moment by moment, trusting Him to pull all the pieces together in His timing. Many times we will have to wait, but when we do so in obedience, God will bless the outcome.

COMPLETE OBEDIENCE: NOAH

When we read about the life of Noah in GENESIS 6–9, we see a clear picture of complete obedience. When God called this man to do something extraordinary—a task that seemed both impossible and illogical—

Noah complied without asking questions. Noah obeyed God despite what other people thought of him. And when we choose the path of obedience, we must likewise be prepared for the negative responses we will undoubtedly receive from others.

Will it always be popular for you to obey God? No, it will not. Will people criticize you? Yes, they probably will. Might they think some things that you do are ridiculous? Yes. Will they sometimes laugh at you? Yes. Noah chose to walk with God in the midst of a corrupt society. In fact, it was so wicked that God chose to destroy every living human being on the face of the earth with the exception of one family. We can only imagine what those evil people must have said to Noah as they watched him day after day.

From the life of Noah, we can deduce an important key to obedience: when God tells us to do something, we must not focus on the circumstances or the persons who would deter us from carrying out God's instructions. If Noah had begun to listen to his critics, he would not have built the ark, and he would have been swept away with the rest of the earth. Instead, he chose to be absolutely obedient to God.

ULTIMATE OBEDIENCE: JESUS

Finally let us consider the life of Jesus. He was perfect—God in human form. We can learn countless lessons from His life. Even though we cannot be perfect and blameless as Christ was, the Holy Spirit enables us to obey God. If this were not possible, God would not be just. Therefore, whatever He requires of us—whether it be painful or joyful, profitable or costly—God Himself will help us to obey.

The God we serve is a gracious, loving, indescribable, awesome God. I know from experience that obedience has to be a priority in every believer's life. It is the only way you will ever become the person God wants you to be, and the only way you will ever achieve the things in life that He has so wonderfully prepared for you.

When you receive Jesus Christ as your Savior, your first act of obedience should be to pray, "Father, forgive me of my sins. I've sinned against You; I've been living in rebellion. I'm asking You to forgive me of my sins, not because I'm so good, but because I believe Your Son, Jesus, paid my sin-debt in full." The moment you do that, the Holy Spirit comes into your heart. And do you know what He comes to do? He comes to enable you to walk obediently before God, in His strength and His power.

My prayer for you—my petition on your behalf—is that you will be obedient to God. That way, you can become the person He wants you to be, do the work He desires of you, bear the fruit He enables you to bear, and receive the blessings He has prepared for you.

THE JOY OF OBEDIENCE

Obedience can be a challenge, especially if we think that we know more about our lives and circumstances than God does. However, obeying God is essential to pleasing Him—not just in times of deep, serious temptation, but in moments of simpler testing as well.

In fact, there is never a time when obedience is unimportant to the Lord. Though it may seem easier to obey Him concerning situations that have been clearly defined in His Word, God requires our obedience in every circumstance. Telling a so-called white lie can be just as detrimental to our spiritual well-being as yielding to a greater temptation such as adultery or stealing. In commanding us to obey Him, God has given us a principle by which to live. He has set a framework for our lives that forms a hedge of protection from evil.

Can you remember the last time you were tempted to do the opposite of what you knew God desired you to do? Deep inside, you probably understood what was right, but a struggle ensued in your mind. The question arose: *Should I obey God and please Him, or disobey Him and hope that He won't notice?* In truth, nothing good can come from disobeying God, and nothing bad can come from obeying Him. When we decide to obey God, we choose the way of wisdom. It also is the way to blessing.

Many people think of obedience only as it pertains to parents raising their children. They think that today's youths need to learn how to be obedient. However, obedience is crucial at every level of maturity. As we grow in our walk with the Lord, obedience becomes a cornerstone to fellowship with God. When we obey Him, He pulls us closer to Himself and teaches us more about His precepts and His personal love.

Ironically, as we grow older, our sensitivity to God's leading sometimes diminishes. We reason that we have learned how to live righteously before God and therefore do not need to dig deeper into the issue of obedience. We judge others when they fail to obey God, but dismiss the issue in our own lives.

That was what the nation of Israel did, as recorded in the book of Judges. The Bible says they did what was right in their own eyes (JUDG. 17:6). In other words, Israel did as it pleased. The people forgot the Lord and served other gods. They made their own decisions, lived immoral lives, and refused to worship the God who, years earlier, had brought them out of Egyptian bondage. Their lives were marked by disobedience, and slowly they sank into an even greater bondage than the one their forefathers had experienced at the hands of Pharaoh.

Disobedience sends a message to the Lord declaring that we know better than He does when it comes to governing our lives. However, our self-assurance evaporates when it comes face-to-face with God's sovereignty. When the prophet Isaiah stood in the presence of the Lord, He cried out, "Woe is me!" at the awesome display of God's glory (ISA. 6:5).

Even Isaiah faced a challenge of obedience. God was looking for someone who would take His word to the people of Israel. As far as Isaiah was concerned, no questions needed to be raised. He had seen God's glory, and obedience was his only choice. Can you imagine how different things would have been if Isaiah had followed his intuition rather than God's directive?

God's concern for us springs from His deep love and devotion. He commands our obedience not because He is a strict taskmaster, but because He knows the effect that disobedience and sin will have on our lives. Satan has a different goal in mind. He knows that if he can entice us to sin, our actions will dishonor the Lord and bring sorrow to the heart of God. Disobedience also has fierce repercussions. Feelings of guilt, shame, and worthlessness are just a few of the emotional consequences. Broken lives, destroyed marriages, and bitter disputes also happen when we disobey. While God's eternal love for us cannot change, our sin certainly disrupts our fellowship with the Savior.

Sin alienates believers from God's blessings. God continues to love us but hates the sin that we have embraced. This alone is enough to bring about the Lord's rebuke, causing estrangement between us and the Savior on whom we depend. In times of disobedience, we become spiritually weak and unable to discern right from wrong. Many times, we are unable to reverse our sinful behavior and thereby sink deeper into its grasp.

God does not leave us hopeless, however. The apostle Paul wrote, "No temptation has overtaken you but such as is common to man; and God is faithful, who will not allow you to be tempted beyond what you are able, but with the temptation will provide the way of escape also, so that you will be able to endure it" (1 COR. 10:13). God has provided all we need in order to say no to temptation. Despite the fact that Satan's enticements lead to fretting, lying, or negative thoughts, God's Word is an infinite resource of truth, hope, and assurance. We do not have to yield to sin, because He is sovereign and is always in control.

In PSALM 139, David wrote,

> My frame was not hidden from You,
> When I was made in secret,
> And skillfully wrought in the depths of the earth;
> Your eyes have seen my unformed substance;
> And in Your book were all written
> The days that were ordained for me. (vv. 15–16)

God stays close to us and is personally involved in all we do. He understands our deepest needs and heartfelt longings.

The book of Deuteronomy chronicles Israel's preparation to enter the promised land. God knew that His people would be tempted to stop worshiping Him and pursue the gods of other nations. He made His will very clear to the Israelites and to Joshua, who led them into the promised land: "See, I am setting before you today a blessing and a curse: the blessing, if you listen to the commandments of the LORD your God, which I am commanding you today; and the curse, if you do not listen to the commandments of the LORD your God, but turn aside from the way which I am commanding you today, by following other gods which you have not known" (DEUT. 11:26–28).

In chapter 28, the Lord said, "Now it shall be, if you diligently obey the LORD your God, being careful to do all His commandments which I command you today, the LORD your God will set you high above all the nations of the earth. All these blessings will come upon you and overtake you if you obey the LORD your God" (vv. 1–2). The rest of this chapter spells out the blessings that will come as a result of Israel's obedience. This same principle is at work in our lives. Obedience leads to blessing, while disobedience leads to disappointment, sorrow, and brokenness.

You begin a life of obedience when you apply the following principles to your life:

TRUST GOD WITH YOUR LIFE AND LEAVE THE CONSEQUENCES TO HIM

There is no way to go wrong if you place your hope and trust in God. He created you, and He loves you with an eternal love. You are His greatest concern, and He will never give you second best (PROV. 3:5–6).

LEARN TO WAIT ON THE LORD

When in doubt, refuse to move ahead unless you know that God is leading you. Not all temptation involves sin as we commonly think of it. When you jump ahead of God and make the decision to act without clear instruction from Him, you are disobeying Him (PS. 27:14; 62:1–8).

LEARN TO MEDITATE ON GOD'S WORD

Prayer and meditation are key elements in resisting temptation. When you saturate your mind with the Word of God, you will gain God's viewpoint concerning your life and situation. Therefore, when temptation comes, you will know right from wrong and can act accordingly. Never underestimate the power of God in your life (JOSH. 6:16–20).

LEARN TO LISTEN TO THE HOLY SPIRIT

Many wonder if God speaks to His people today. The answer is yes. He speaks to us through His Word, by His Spirit, and in the counsel of a pastor or a trusted Christian friend. Actually the Spirit of God is the One who draws us to Scripture and points out passages that God seeks to use in our lives. However, we must be sensitive to His voice, or we will miss what He is saying to us. Seek Him through His Word, and spend time with Him by praying and studying the principles written in Scripture.

BE WILLING TO WALK AWAY WHEN THE PATH IS UNCERTAIN

Obedience to God will require you to be firm if you desire to please Him above all others. If you do not sense clear guidance for your situation, ask God to confirm His will to you in His Word. He will never go against Scripture. His intentions for your life always will line up perfectly with what is written in the Bible (NUM. 23:19).

BE WILLING TO EXPERIENCE CONFLICT

Even after Israel entered the promised land, they had to continue driving the enemy out. God rarely empties our lives of trouble and conflict. If He did, our dependence on Him would fade. He allows enough difficulty to keep us turned toward Him (JOHN 16:33). Many times, your obedience will not be viewed as popular, especially if you take a certain stand against the peer pressure of the world. But it will put you in a favorable position before God, and just as He promised to bless the nation of Israel, He will do the same for you.

ACCEPT GOD'S DISCIPLINE WITH THANKSGIVING

When you do disobey God, realize that at any point, you can turn back to Him. The story of the prodigal son told by Jesus (LUKE 15:11–32) is especially significant. In it we read of God's love and forgiveness toward us. While the consequences of sin are unavoidable, we can experience true forgiveness and renewed hope when we turn back to God. Perhaps you have made a wrong decision. You wonder what the outcome will be. Apart from God, the outcome is always eventually sorrow and grief. However, God does not want this for your life. He may not remove all the heartache and pain your decision has caused, but He can forgive you and restore His blessing in your life. When we turn to Him in repentance, He will wash sin's darkness from our lives so that we become white and pure as snow (PS. 51:7).

OBEDIENCE BRINGS BLESSINGS

We never lose when we obey God. Nevertheless, obedience is not easy. Many times it is difficult to understand. But even in times when adversity strikes and nothing makes sense, our best option is one of obedience to God. David learned this principle, and God blessed him greatly. Even when Saul's jealous rage threatened to end David's life, the future king refused to sin against the Lord by taking revenge against his enemy. Committed to obeying God, David would not allow his feelings to shift in a destructive, self-centered direction.

There are times in every Christian's life when, from our human perspective, God's requests seem unreasonable. When this happens, we must remember that He sees the entirety of our lives. He knows the plans He has for us and exactly what it will take to reach His goal of molding us into the image of His Son: "'For I know the plans that I have for you,' declares the LORD, 'plans for welfare and not for calamity to give you a future and a hope'" (JER. 29:11).

Jesus Christ is our greatest example of obedience. He obeyed God even to the point of death so that we might have eternal life. There is no greater obedience than this. Like Jesus, when we obey, we declare our dependency on God. We also demonstrate that we are willing to submit our lives to Him and trust Him for the future. Even though we may not understand why we are faced with a sudden trial or when an open door of opportunity has closed, our first and last response always needs to be obedience.

There have been times in my life when I found that I was standing at a crossroads. Deep within my heart, I knew that the only way to continue was to be obedient to the Lord—not just partially, but completely.

FIRST SAMUEL 15:22 tells us, "To obey is better than sacrifice." What are you facing today that is tempting you to disobey God? Whatever it is, it is not worth missing out on His fellowship and His plans for your life. When you choose to obey God, you have chosen the way to hope and blessing.

SUGGESTED BIBLE READING

JOHN 14:23; 16:33; LUKE 5:1–11; 19:17; GENESIS 1:28; 2:17; 3:3; 6–9; 2 CORINTHIANS 10:5; 1 SAMUEL 10:8; 13:10–14; 15:22; ISAIAH 6:5; PSALMS 27:14; 51:7; 62:1–8; 139; DEUTERONOMY 11:26–28; PROVERBS 3:5–6; JOSHUA 6:16–20; LUKE 15:11–32; and JEREMIAH 29:11.

PRAYER

Dear Father in heaven, I ask Your forgiveness for my self-sufficiency and for all the times I hear Your commands yet fail to obey them. I purpose to align my life with Your principles and to obey Your Word. Please help me in this pursuit and convict me when I stray. Amen.

JOURNAL QUESTIONS

- Is there an area of your life in which you do not obey God?

_____

_____

_____

_____

_____

- Can you make a commitment today to obey the Lord and trust Him?

_____

_____

_____

_____

_____

- If possible, find an accountability partner to help you with areas in which you struggle.

_____

_____

_____

_____

Obedience may rarely be easy, but it is always worth it.
Learn more about the value of faithful obedience to God at
www.InTouch.org.

PRINCIPLE
6

KNOWING GOD'S WILL IS
WORTH THE WAIT

Waiting on God's timing is one of the most profitable lessons I have ever learned. I have petitioned God on many occasions and received virtual silence as an answer. At times, the wait for a response to my prayers seemed to go on forever. But however long the wait, He has always come through in the end.

Waiting is probably one of the most difficult things that Christians are called to do. This is especially true when there is something that seems to be right at our fingertips and we think that God is about to bless us with the desires of our hearts.

My daughter, Becky, learned this lesson when she was just twenty-one years old—in fact, we learned it together. She had become engaged to a wonderful young man. I could not point out a single thing wrong with him. He had a wonderful family, and they all loved my daughter as much as he did. But something deep within my spirit told me that her marriage to him wasn't right. I had no explanation for my feelings, but I couldn't deny them either.

One evening we were sitting around the dinner table talking about the wedding, and I began to pray silently, asking the Lord if I should reveal my concerns to Becky. I looked across the table at her, overcome with feelings of love and responsibility. I knew I had my daughter's heart in my hand, and it was as if God said to me, *You must tell her what you feel, or you'll live the rest of your life wishing you had.*

The words spilled from my mouth: "Becky, would you like me to help you call off the wedding?" She was as stunned as I. "Daddy! What are you talking about?" she said. I said, "Becky, I don't know. I just felt impressed by God to ask you that question." She was very quiet for a few heavy moments; then we started talking again. I said, "Becky, if you could do anything that you wanted to do at this point in your life, what would you do?" She hardly even hesitated: "I would go to seminary." I said, "Okay, that's what you should do. I believe that's what God wants you to do, and that's what we're going to plan on." Then I reassured her, "If you'll wait for God, He'll bring the right person in your life. As fine as this young man is, I don't believe he's the right person."

When we finished our meal, my faithful daughter telephoned her fiancé and informed him of her new plans. He responded by demeaning her choice, saying the last thing he should have said: "How long are you going to listen to your daddy?" When she heard that, her decision was confirmed.

That whole process was very difficult for both of us. It was one of those critical times in my life when I knew that I had to obey God and be totally misunderstood or be loved forever. As always, God rewarded my obedience. That fall, Becky joined her brother, Andy, at Dallas Seminary. After a period of waiting, the Lord blessed her with a wonderful husband—this one was the perfect match. She couldn't be happier with her family.

God always has a very clear reason for telling us to wait, and the reason is without exception to our benefit. Waiting is essential in living the

Christian life, walking in obedience to God, and receiving the best of God's blessings.

King David certainly knew what it meant to wait upon the Lord. You may recall that David was only sixteen years old when he was anointed king. Yet he did not take the throne until he was thirty years of age. So, he had to wait almost fifteen years. Now, how many times do you suppose David said, "Lord, You haven't forgotten me, have You?" God's plan did come to pass, but David was made to wait quite a while. This is why you read in Scripture that David again and again waited upon the Lord. He learned the hard way—running from King Saul, being chased, hiding in caves, and facing persecution of many kinds. If you had asked him, "Well, David, did you learn your lesson?" he would have replied, "Yes, but after many, many, many failures."

Being patient is surely difficult, but failing to wait upon the Lord can bring about disastrous consequences. First, when we do not wait, we get out of God's will. Second, we delay God's planned blessing for us. Because we move ahead of His steps, we get out of cycle and miss God's blessings in His time. Third, we bring pain and suffering upon others and ourselves. Throughout Scripture, you can see the resulting pain that people endure from getting out of God's will and doing things their own way. Fourth, we are prone to make snap judgments that quite often turn out to cost us dearly in terms of finances, emotional energy, and/or relationships.

I can think of far too many stories that did not end as happily as Becky's. Throughout my years of ministry, I have seen a number of young people who were eager to move ahead in their careers. Some of them were willing to pay the price of apprenticeship and work their way to the top one step at a time. Others barreled ahead before they were mature enough to assume the responsibilities of a more demanding position. In doing so, they not only frustrated their own ambitions, but they caused discord among those with whom they worked. Trying to bypass necessary steps in professional development and trampling anyone who stands in your way will not help you to get ahead more quickly. You may get the promotion or title you are seeking, but in the end you will sacrifice far too much for it.

I can't think of anyone I saw step out ahead of God, trying to grab more than his share, who didn't leave the ministry angry, disillusioned, or worse. I have literally watched people ruin their careers and their families trying to move ahead too quickly. Their demise is predictable and sad.

Many people are not willing to wait on God for His timing, particularly when it involves the possibility of letting go of something they desire desperately. I have often counseled couples whom I felt were not ready to marry, and I always exhorted them to wait. Some did and some didn't. I'll never forget the expression on the face of a young girl I had advised against marriage. I'd explained the reasons for my concern, and she had promised not to marry, but did so anyway. A few years after her wedding, I saw her sobbing in the foyer outside my study. When our eyes met, she came in and told me they were divorcing.

A lot of people make this mistake. They just can't wait for God's timing. They think, *I'm thirty-five years old, and if I don't get married now, I'll be single forever.* Fear grips them, and they think they will lose what they desire if they don't grab it as quickly as they can. They fear losing an opportunity that will never again present itself. But in reality, they end up making mistakes that last forever. Instead of wanting what God wants in God's timing, they want what they want in their own timing. When we take our eyes off God and try to manipulate our situation to conform to our will, we usually make a colossal mess of things. Whenever we reach for something that is not of God, it turns to ashes. He will never prosper what we manipulate. No matter how hard we try, it just doesn't work. Either we can repent, back off, and wait for the Lord—in which case, more than likely, He'll give us what we ask for—or we can step out ahead of Him and lose it.

Something may be the will of God, but if you step out ahead of His timing, you can ruin His blessing for your life. Think of it this way: if you assemble a model airplane that you intend to fly, you must first wait for the glue to dry before launching your aircraft. Let's suppose you have waited for two hours and the glue looks as if it is nearly dry. It's not quite solid, but you're eager to get going, so you take your newly minted flying machine outside and hoist it into the air. Before it even gains altitude, it comes crashing to the ground, pieces falling everywhere. The same analogy can be made for nearly every aspect of life: eating a half-baked pie that hasn't stayed in the oven long enough, pulling a vegetable from the garden before it's ripe, running a race when you haven't trained enough. The law of waiting governs much of the universe, and we live more happily when we learn to obey with grace.

LEARNING THE ART OF ACTIVE WAITING

Waiting on the Lord does not mean being stagnant. God is moving and active. He has a definite plan for your life, but He may be calling you to wait awhile, for what purpose I do not know. I pray that you can discover that for yourself, in His time.

Timing is everything. You see it in war—attacking at the wrong moment could cost the battle. You see it in the operating room—too fast, too short, too much, too little, or too late would be a tragedy. You see it in sports, wherein a delay could mean the loss of the game. Of all the things in which timing is important, however, it is in your daily walk with the Lord and in your decision-making processes that timing is crucial.

One of the primary reasons that believers step out of God's will—and out of fellowship with the Lord—is that they step out on their own without His blessing or guidance. They are eager and impatient about achieving something they are convinced will please Him. Without waiting for clear direction, they move ahead and make decisions apart from understanding the will and purpose of God. It is important for you to realize what it means to truly wait upon the Lord.

First, waiting upon the Lord does not require you to be idle. Instead, it simply means pausing until you receive further instructions. You should think of waiting as a determined stillness, during which time you decide not to act until the Lord gives clear direction.

However, because this is an instant-gratification generation, people want to do things now, get things now, and move ahead. Yet there are many, many verses in Scripture about waiting upon the Lord. Sometimes when you step ahead of Him, God will bless you to some degree, but it certainly is not going to be God's best. Furthermore, you may make a big mistake for which you could be very sorry.

God has a plan for your life. That plan is clearly directed from the outset. That is, God does not leave you to guess. God works this way because all of His plans are connected, and He knows that what you do will affect other people as well as yourself, both now and in the future. It is essential that you listen to Him and wait.

Second, in Scripture God often instructs His people to wait. For example, read PSALM 27:14: "Wait for the LORD; be strong and let your heart take courage; yes, wait for the LORD." Sometimes it takes a great deal of courage to wait and wait as you start to think, *If I don't take advantage of this opportunity now, I'm going to miss it.* Yet God says, "Let your heart take courage; yes, wait for the LORD."

Also notice PSALM 37:4–7:

Delight yourself in the LORD;
And He will give you the desires of your heart.
Commit your way to the LORD,
Trust also in Him, and He will do it.
He will bring forth your righteousness as the light

And your judgment as the noonday.
Rest in the LORD and wait patiently for Him.

The only way to wait patiently is to rest in Him; you must trust Him to the point that you are no longer anxious. Clearly, then, you cannot separate waiting upon the Lord and trusting in Him; these two things go hand in hand.

Third, your waiting should be marked by silence:

My soul, wait in silence for God only,
For my hope is from Him.
He only is my rock and my salvation,
My stronghold; I shall not be shaken. (PS. 62:5–6)

How often do you find yourself waiting and yet not being very silent about it? Oftentimes, you may wait but complain about it; other times, you may wait but tell God why you think He ought to hurry up. Would you agree that most of the time, God is a little too slow for your schedule? Yet "my soul waits in silence for God only" (PS. 62:1). Remember, waiting and trusting are inseparable. You must trust enough to wait in silence.

Fourth, God will strengthen you through your waiting. See the promise in ISAIAH 40:31, which you may know by heart:

Yet those who wait for the LORD
Will gain new strength;
They will mount up with wings like eagles,
They will run and not get tired,
They will walk and not become weary.

God wants you to learn how to do that. The wind beneath your wings is your trust in God. If you trust in Him, then He will help you shoulder the weight of your burdens. Does that mean that you will never get weary? No, of course not. It is one thing to be tired *in* your labors; it is something else to be tired *of* your labors, which is to become weary on the inside. You can go a long way even though you may be weary on the outside. However, when you have no one in whom to trust, your spirit becomes weary, and that is a far worse predicament.

Fortunately God promises us that when we wait upon the Lord, He will renew our strength. We will mount up with wings like eagles and soar. Not only that, but He says we will run and not grow weary, walk and not lose heart. God has provided all the strength and energy that we need.

Fifth, waiting does not involve looking around to see what others are doing. How often have you been sure of what the Lord has said to do, but then changed your course of action because of what you saw others doing around you? Or how often have you been sure of what the Lord has said, but then begun to doubt Him because of the negative voices you heard?

When it comes to your personal, private walk with God, this is the bottom line: Are you going to listen to God and do what He says? Are you going to wait upon Him when your peers become impatient and every-thing around you is pushing you to move?

Waiting demands patience, and it certainly requires trust. As you wait upon the Lord, you will have to stand strong against the pressure of other people who want to goad you into making a decision that fits their schedules and timing. Maybe you are in a relationship or a job and don't feel ready to move ahead. If God has not given you the green light, moving forward at the insistence of others is the worst thing you can do.

Yes, waiting is hard. It is difficult to stand still when everything in you wants to move. However, wise men and women wait upon the Lord until they have heard from Him. Then, when they finally move, it is with boldness, confidence, courage, strength, and absolute assurance that God will keep His word.

WHEN GOD DOESN'T SEEM TO ANSWER

There are times in every Christian's life when God seems distant and un-interested in the circumstances. We pray and diligently seek His will, but our need, at least from our perspective, remains unmet. We wait and wait but do not hear from the Lord. Does God truly have an answer? Does He care when we hurt and struggle against the pressures of life? How should we handle times of spiritual silence when we feel as though He is standing at a distance and is not going to answer our prayers according to our desires?

The best way to understand God's heart is by studying the principles found in His Word. Before you decide this will *not* work for you or your situation, take a few moments to read the story of Mary, Martha, and Lazarus. Each of these people had definite needs. Lazarus needed a healing touch from God. He was deathly ill (JOHN 11:1), and Jesus had the power to heal him. Mary and Martha had tremendous needs. How would they survive without Lazarus? Not only was he their brother; he also was their financial provider. He was the head of their household, and because they were not married, Lazarus took care of them. Jesus knew that.

In fact, the Lord was their close friend and a frequent guest in their home. Bethany, where Lazarus and his sisters lived, was not far from Jerusalem. Once Mary and Martha realized that the sickness of their brother could lead to death, it only seemed right to send for Jesus. They knew the power that God had given Him. Their appeal to the Lord was one of love and friendship: "Lord, behold, he whom You love is sick" (JOHN 11:3).

The issue in this story is not one of healing—it is one of need and how God met that need. God has the power to heal every disease. The issue that confronts us in a situation like this one is God's will versus our will. We are taught to pray and to ask God to meet our needs. But there is something deep within this process that the Father wants us to learn. We begin to understand just how committed He is to meeting our needs when we learn to accept His will as being perfect. We also must acknowledge that His timing is right, just as His strength is sufficient and His love is eternal. Sometimes when we have to wait for God's provision or answer, it seems as if He is completely uninterested in our situation.

As their brother lay dying, Mary and Martha did not understand how deeply involved God was in their lives. More than likely, we have at times failed to understand this reality as well. However, Jesus was determined to demonstrate His intimate care for these women and for His friend Lazarus. But first, Mary and Martha would have to wait. Their prayers, though in harmony with God's will, would appear to go unanswered.

Many times we lose patience with God and attempt to meet our own unmet needs. In so doing, we often make matters worse by resorting to the following:

DENIAL

We tell ourselves there is not a problem. While denial is an initial defense we use to protect ourselves from the reality of deep tragedy, a prolonged period of denial is not healthy. We need to face reality with God, knowing that He has a solution for the problems we encounter.

AVOIDANCE

We distance ourselves from the problem in an attempt to protect ourselves from further pain. Avoidance works for a short time. We can see how God used it in the lives of His saints to provide brief intervals of rest. However, just like denial, avoidance prevents us from dealing with the problem. The solution is to seek God for wisdom and a precise way to handle our circumstances, even if this includes waiting for Him to lead us beyond this moment in time. Be willing to wait for God's best. Jumping ahead of Him leads only to more confusion.

PROJECTION

We use projection when we blame others. Mary and Martha were quick to tell Jesus, "If you had been here, my brother would not have died" (JOHN 11:21, 32). God is completely aware of your situation. He knows exactly what you are facing, and He knows how you will react. This is why it is crucial for you to turn to Him for wisdom and for the right response. Accept responsibility for your life and the problems you are facing. Lazarus's illness was a fact of life and not a form of punishment. God sometimes uses painful circumstances to mold our lives.

LYING

When we avoid telling the truth, we end up hurting others and ourselves. There is only one way to handle the trials of life, and that is truthfully. We do not have to disclose all we know or feel, however. God wants us to be careful with our words. Lying and rationalization do not help solve the problem. They only hinder a final, godly resolution.

GIVING IN AND GIVING UP

Usually when trials come, we are faced with the temptation to quit. Discouragement is one of Satan's favorite forms of attack. He believes that if he can discourage us, we will give up and turn away from God's will and plan for our lives.

Never give up! Trust God to the end, and you will see His goodness become a reality in your life.

CONFORMITY

Rather than stand for what we know is right, we can easily conform to the situation under pressure. Our initiative and creativity drain away, and we run the risk of sinking into depression.

Mary and Martha might have been tempted to fall into self-pity and doubt, but they did not yield to either of these. When Jesus arrived in Bethany, Martha met Him with these words: "Lord, if You had been here, my brother would not have died. Even now I know that whatever You ask of God, God will give You" (JOHN 11:21–22). How did the sisters deal with the fact that Jesus did not rush to their dying brother's side? We are not given their immediate response, but they were probably disappointed. After all, they loved their brother.

GOD'S TIMING

Somewhere along the line, Mary and Martha had to deal with the sovereignty of God. They had to come to a point where they accepted God's will over their own wills. Each one of us will face this decision at some time. We may wonder why, on the surface, it appears that God has not met our needs. Yet deep inside we should understand that God never leaves us hopeless. He has a plan and a design for our lives that are well fitted for every trial, sorrow, heartache, or problem we face.

Jesus had predetermined that He would heal Lazarus, but He would do it in such a way that He alone would be glorified. He also would accomplish His will in the lives of Mary and Martha. They would come to a place of acceptance.

HOW SHOULD YOU HANDLE YOUR UNMET NEEDS?

BEGIN WITH PRAYER. LET YOUR NEEDS BE MADE KNOWN TO GOD (PHIL. 4:6)

Jesus taught His disciples that prayer is a lifestyle, not just an activity in which you participate. When you feel overwhelmed by your circumstances, prayer is the one way to change the direction of your mind and heart. It places your focus on God, who is the only Source of hope and truth.

ACKNOWLEDGE YOUR NEED AND THE BURDEN THAT YOU ARE CARRYING

The saints of the church used an endearing phrase when they talked about giving their problems to God in prayer. They said, "Roll your burden over onto the Lord." This is your hope: Jesus never fails. His compassions are "new every morning" (LAM. 3:23), and they are specifically designed to help you bear up under the pressure that comes from trial, tragedy, and sorrow.

CLAIM GOD'S PROMISES

When you are facing a difficult situation, train yourself to appropriate divine promises. Scripture is your greatest source of encouragement. Resist the temptation to run to several people seeking verification for what God has required you to do. Faith is a strong anchor that holds you steady when emotional gale-force winds strike. Claiming God's promises and remaining committed to the course He has given you is a powerful way to face any tribulation or change.

SEEK GOD'S DIRECTION

You can do this through the study of His Word and through prayer. Ask Him to help you distinguish between the real need and what you perceive as a need. You may think you have a specific need, but it is actually a desire. Many times, if God gave you what you wanted, you would drift in your devotion to Him. Make sure that your motives are pure and God-centered rather than self-centered.

Also, pray that the Lord will show you exactly where you are missing His best. If there are walls that you have erected, you will not easily be able to accept His will for your life. Ask Him to tear down any barriers that separate you from Him. Once you let go and allow Him to meet your needs according to His timing and plan, you will discover His goodness and grace flowing into every area of your life.

BE WILLING TO WAIT

This is crucial. Mary and Martha had to wait. Their hope had faded—their brother was dead. Jesus did not come when they sent for Him. But God had a grander purpose in mind than just meeting their expectation. He would demonstrate His power to bring new life to a dead man. What was the greater miracle: healing Lazarus or bringing him back to life after he was dead for four days? Of course, his resurrection was the more stunning feat. This miracle also pointed to the future resurrection of Christ. God always has a greater good in mind. Many times our spiritual insight is limited, but God sees all. He knows exactly what is transpiring on every spiritual level, along with all that we are facing. He has a plan, and if we are wise, we will wait for Him to reveal it to us.

THANK GOD IN ADVANCE FOR HIS PROVISION

Positive confession is a powerful force in the life of a believer. This does not mean talking boastfully or claiming God's deliverance apart from His expressed will for your life. Thanking God for His faithfulness and provision is an indication of your submission to His will regardless of your hopes or expectations. Seasons of life may not turn out the way you thought. You may struggle. Mary and Martha watched as their brother died. However, because we serve a risen Lord and Savior, we know that no matter what we face in this life, God will ultimately deliver us from all evil. He will bless us as we seek to know Him intimately. He will guard, protect, and lead us into a place of great blessing and hope.

Have you trusted the Savior with your unmet needs, or are you still focused on satisfying your hopes and desires as quickly as possible? Only God can completely meet your needs. Trust Him—give Him your burden to carry and you will witness a tremendous miracle. And if you have to be patient, the very act of waiting will strengthen your hope and breathe new life into your being.

WHY IS IT WISE TO WAIT?

1. TO RECEIVE GOD'S CLEAR DIRECTION FOR YOUR LIFE

Can you name anything you should not share with God? Talking to Him, listening to Him, waiting upon Him . . . everything deserves His attention. The Lord desires you to sift everything through His will, purpose, plan, and Word.

2. TO KEEP IN STEP WITH GOD'S TIMING

Often, what you want for yourself is also what God wants for you. However, your timing may not be the same as His. So, even though God intends for you to have a blessing, He may withhold it for a time and say, "No, this is not the right time to proceed."

3. TO ALLOW GOD THE PROPER TIME TO PREPARE YOU FOR HIS ANSWER

Very often, you may know exactly what God wants for you. However, He may tell you to wait. You may cry, "But if this is what I'm supposed to have, why can't I have it now?" The answer is that sometimes God has to prepare you for the blessing or the next move. What would be a delight for you tomorrow might be an absolute disaster today.

4. TO STRENGTHEN YOUR FAITH IN HIM

Think about how Abraham felt. God had promised a son, but decades passed without a child. Had Abraham heard God incorrectly? No, because we know that Abraham became the father of the entire Hebrew nation. Abraham was not perfect, but through years of waiting he learned to trust the Lord.

5. TO ALLOW GOD TO SIFT THROUGH YOUR MOTIVES TO REVEAL YOUR DESIRES

Even if what you want meshes with what God wants, your motives may be poorly aligned. What is your motive? Is it something selfish? Is it really what you believe God wants for your life? God often makes His people wait so that He may take time to clean their hearts of poor motives.

After fifty years of listening to people's frustrations with Christianity, I am fully persuaded there is one primary, underlying cause for their dissatisfaction. They do not understand the nature of God's will or how to discern it. Without that knowledge—which affects every aspect of life from prayer to decision making—they can never know where they are in the Christian journey.

When people are unsure of God's direction, they often think, *I will just do my best and hope it all works out.* But that is not *God's* best. He has a will—that is, a specific plan, purpose, and desire—for every one of His children. JEREMIAH 29:11–13 clearly shows that His plan is for our good, and we can discover it if we wholeheartedly seek it. Remember that God is a Creator, not a reactor. He planned the creation and the nation of Israel. Old Testament prophecies make us aware of events He mapped out from the beginning. What's more, He designed every detail of the Messiah's arrival, as well as our redemption, resurrection, and rewards. After such precise planning, God would never tell humanity, "Just do the best you can." We could never fulfill His unique plan for us individually if left to our own devices.

God is sovereign; His determined will encompasses all situations. The events in His divine program are absolutely inevitable, immutable, and irresistible. At the same time, our Savior allows our free will to play a part in our lives. Scripture spells out certain aspects of His desired will so that we can wisely choose His best. For example, the Bible tells us that God wants us to know His plan and purpose for our lives. Paul wrote to the Colossians: "For this reason also, since the day we heard of it, we have not ceased to pray for you and to ask that you may be filled with the knowledge of His will in all spiritual wisdom and understanding" (Col. 1:9).

God does not withhold any information we need regarding His will, but we cannot expect Him to reveal the next ten years of our lives now. Since He wants us to live in trusting dependence upon Him each and every day, He does not show us too far ahead what He is going to do—His Word is a lamp to our feet, not a floodlight to illuminate the highway clear through to our destination (Ps. 119:105). God knew that if we had a book telling about our whole lives, we would read it, close it, and walk away trusting in our own strength. Instead, He desires that you and I know and obey His will for us day by day.

KNOWING GOD'S WILL

As a pastor, I hear this common question: "How can I know the will of God?" People ask this not only when they're trying to determine the over-all direction their lives should take, but also regarding smaller, daily decisions. Many are confused about whether it is possible to know the Father's will or if He even has a specific will for their lives.

Be assured: you *can* know God's will, and you can know it for *sure*. God does not play games with His children by hiding His thoughts from us. One of His greatest desires for us is that we live out His plan for our lives. And yet people often agonize about whether or not they have some-how stepped outside of God's will or are missing the mark without know-ing it.

You do not have to fret, because you can know with complete cer-tainty God's will for every circumstance of your life. Although He may not disclose every detail about each situation, His Word reveals very specific steps you can take each day in order to learn and fulfill His will for your life.

In his letter to the Colossian church, Paul wrote that he was praying for them to be "filled with the knowledge of [God's] will" (COL. 1:9), not simply to have some vague idea about what the Lord had in mind. To be filled with this knowledge means that the will of God permeates every single aspect of what we think, do, and say. His will is to be the grid through which we sift each motivation, action, and circumstance. In other words, no matter what we are involved in—whether it concerns family, finances, relationships, health, or faith—our continual thought should be, *Father, what would You have me to do? What is the wise course of action?* Unless we know and follow God's will, we are going to miss the wondrous blessings He has in store for us.

In order to discern what God desires for you, it is helpful to understand that His will has two aspects. First, His *determined* will includes those things that are unchangeable—God's overruling sovereignty will see to it that nothing deters these occurrences. Fulfillment of prophecy and divine promises are examples of His determined will. Second, His *desired* will involves everything He wants for you that, with your limited free will, you are able to turn down. Both aspects of God's will represent His very best for you.

The benefits of following God's will—and the consequences of ignoring it—are compelling reasons to search out what the Lord desires for your life. When making important decisions, consider the following questions:

1. IS IT CONSISTENT WITH THE WORD OF GOD?

Look for Scripture that either indicates this is the right way to go or gives you reason not to proceed. Even if you cannot find verses describing a situation comparable to yours, look for applicable truths. God's Word is full of life principles; a single passage can offer wisdom that applies to many circumstances. Consider PSALM 119:11: "Your word I have treasured in my heart, that I may not sin against You." In other words, Scripture is a guide, but if it is to be useful, you must read it, and you must store its wisdom in your heart.

2. Is This a Wise Decision?

To answer this question, you must ask yourself several others: *What are the future consequences? Am I rushing into something? Where is this going to take me? Will it create debt? Will it harm anyone?* As you begin to ask these questions, the Holy Spirit will bear witness to your spirit whether moving ahead is right or wrong. But answer these questions honestly—Satan wants to help program your mind so that you will rationalize and conclude that what you want to do is okay.

3. Can I Honestly Ask God to Enable Me to Achieve This?

Some people will tell you it is okay to ask God for anything, but that is not the case. For example, even if you need money badly, you cannot ask God to permit a deceptive or fraudulent scheme. Remember, anything you acquire outside of God's will sooner or later turns to ashes.

4. Do I Have Genuine Peace About This?

Colossians 3:15 declares, "Let the peace of Christ rule in your hearts." But what does it mean to have peace? Some people "pray" about their decisions without giving God an opportunity to respond. They simply talk about their desires and assume they have a divine go-ahead, but that is not seeking the mind of God. You cannot force peace, but you can know when it is genuine. As you lie down at night and have a moment to be still, bring your concern before the Lord. If there isn't a ripple in your heart, your conscience and emotions are saying yes, and you understand God to be saying yes, then you have perfect peace. Should you sense anything else, stop and wait.

Sometimes what you desire is actually in God's will, but not for the present moment. Until His timing is right, you will not experience peace about proceeding. An answer of "no" or "wait" might seem frustrating if you desperately want something. But think about how safe we are as believers. God will never lie to us or mislead us. He will always guide us in the direction that is in our best interest, and we need to be wise enough to follow. He simply will not give us any peace about something that is not His will—if He did, we would not be able to trust Him.

5. DOES THIS FIT WHO I AM AS A FOLLOWER OF JESUS?

Some things just do not fit a child of God. For example, the Bible says that the body is the temple of the Holy Spirit (1 COR. 6:19), so anything that is physically harmful is not the will of God. Divine discipline comes in different ways; if we disobey the laws of health, we will suffer the consequences, even though we are obedient in other ways. Another area of concern is the believer's testimony. The way we respond to other people— whether they are family, coworkers, or waiters serving our meal—should be consistent with the fact that we belong to Christ and reflect Him to the world. In other words, if we claim to be Christians, it would not be fitting to hold a grudge, gossip, have inappropriate relationships, or express unduly harsh criticism.

6. DOES THIS FIT GOD'S OVERALL PLAN FOR MY LIFE?

We need to consider how our thinking, conduct, and here-and-now decisions coincide with the Lord's long-range plans for us. This is why we must teach our children to be very careful about how they decide upon a vocation, choose a marriage partner, and make all the other major decisions of life. In each instance, the question is, *Does this fit God's purpose for my life?* It would be one thing if the Lord left all choices up to us; then we would be free to make every decision without considering His will on the matter. But He has a specific plan for each of His children, and it is for our best because He is a loving, all-knowing, all-wise Father.

7. WILL THIS DECISION HONOR GOD?

That is, *Am I showing respect and reverence for the heavenly Father by taking this course of action? Is it evident by what I am doing that I acknowl-*

edge Jesus Christ as the Lord and Master of my life? Our actions and attitudes should be in keeping with who we know God to be rather than a statement that we are "doing our own thing." Our disobedience grieves the heart of God, but He is not the only One who notices. The world watches Christians to see if we are consistent or hypocritical, so it is important that our decisions reflect an obedient heart toward the Lord.

Considered honestly, these seven questions reveal a lot about what is in your heart, and they also help you to discover the heart of God. Once you know God's mind on a matter, there is one final question to ask yourself: *Now that I know His will, am I willing to do it?* Following the Lord can be costly (LUKE 14:26–33)—you may be misunderstood, criticized, or penalized in some way. But no matter what God may see fit to do with your life, it is always the best possible course of action. By obeying Him and watching Him work, you will see how faithful He is.

If you are in the process of making a difficult decision and are frightened about the consequences, remember that you have entrusted your life to a loving heavenly Father who plans only the best, promises only the best, and provides only the best. You simply cannot lose when you obey the will of God.

SUGGESTED BIBLE READING

Psalms 27:14; 37:4–7; 62; 119:11, 105; John 11:1–22; Lamentations 3:23; Jeremiah 29:11–13; Colossians 1:9; 3:15; 1 Corinthians 6:19; and Luke 14:26–33.

PRAYER

Lord, I pray that You will teach me how to wait on You for Your perfect timing. I turn over to You all of my expectations and trust that You will bring about what is best for me at the right time. Amen.

JOURNAL QUESTIONS

- Can you think of a time when you stepped out ahead of God's timing?

_____

_____

_____

_____

_____

- Are you waiting for God to do something in your life right now?

_____

_____

_____

_____

_____

- Practice active waiting by praying, reading Scripture, and sharing your experience with Christian loved ones who can wait with you.

How can you know God is active when you pray, even if He delays His answer? Discover the value of biblical prayer and patience at _www.InTouch.org_ today.

PRINCIPLE
7

GOD REFINES US BY FIRE

Cloth can dust off a piece of gold, but the metal must be refined to remove embedded impurities. That is, it must be melted by fire so that any tarnish or pollution can rise and be skimmed from the surface.

The Christian life is frequently compared to this process: "He will . . . refine them like gold and silver, so that they may present to the LORD offerings in righteousness" (MAL. 3:3). When we face struggles, God is refining us like precious metal, digging deep into our lives to eliminate all the dirt and pollution. He does this not to hurt us, but to help us grow into beautiful reflections of Him.

Too often we hear people exclaim, "This world is out of control!" Those with little or no belief in an almighty God of the universe find themselves without any source of strength or encouragement when their world begins to collapse. Family heartache, financial problems, or national tragedies—these are all things that we have witnessed firsthand. In the face of such turmoil, how can we be sure that God is in control?

If I had to choose a single book in Scripture that powerfully reveals God's complete control on page after page from beginning to end, it would be Genesis. In this first book of the Bible, we get to see God working through all types of circumstances and obstacles. The first one, as revealed in the first chapter of Genesis, was absolute nothingness. Think about that for a moment. God created *everything that is . . .* out of *nothing at all.* Therefore, He is the supreme Lord over creation.

Next, in the chapter 3, we see that sin invaded God's perfect creation. Did this show God's lack of control? No, because in spite of the presence of sin in the world, He provided a way for you and me to conquer sin and death and achieve victory.

Third, chapters 6–7 reveal that mankind was so vile, so wicked, and so evil that God decided to destroy every single person on earth with a great flood. Did this show God's lack of control? No, because in His power, the Lord saved one family to repopulate the earth—a family to be the means by which all people could later be blessed through Christ Jesus.

Fourth, after the floodwaters subsided and the population again began to grow, God wanted the people to scatter, but instead, they chose to stay together in one place. They even built a tower to reach into the heavens so that they could feel close to the Lord. Did this show God's lack of control? No, because God stepped in, confused their languages, and thereby scattered them all over the globe. He did not allow their actions to cancel His plans for them.

Again and again throughout Genesis, we see this pattern: God plans to do something, and despite human unfaithfulness, His perfect will is accomplished. This is the case throughout all of Scripture, and it is still true today. God is in control despite our pain, questions, turmoil, and selfishness.

GOD IS IN CONTROL

I remember a particular time when I was struggling with discouragement, doubt, fear, and loneliness. I spent many evenings having long conversations with a close friend to whom I poured out my heart for hours. Many times during these talks, my friend stopped me and said, "But remember, God is in control." This statement became an anchor in my life. No matter how hard the winds blew or how much the adversity intensified, my soul remained anchored to the simple truth: God is in control. I discovered that when a person is able to face terrifying obstacles with the assurance of God's complete control, an awesome sense of power and assurance begins to well up inside his heart.

The psalmist David learned this lesson through ups and downs, successes and fierce challenges. David praised God for His dominion, crying out, "The LORD has established His throne in the heavens; and His sovereignty rules over all" (Ps. 103:19). David—Israel's most beloved king—recognized his humble submission to the One who sits on the heavenly throne, the Lord of all creation.

David also introduced us to a vital aspect of God's character, His complete *sovereignty*. What do we mean by sovereignty? This word denotes God's supreme and absolute rule, control, and authority over this entire universe and every single human being. In this, He is all-powerful, all-knowing, and all-present.

Many people in this world either deny God's existence or try to excuse Him from responsibility when bad things happen. In effect, even those who may seek to defend God are saying, "God exists, but He didn't allow that. That happened without His consent." These people do not realize that they are insulting and rejecting His complete sovereignty over all aspects of life.

Why do they do this? Why do they seem to stumble over or overlook God's sovereignty? First, it is clear that many do not understand the Word of God, which clearly teaches God's complete control over creation. Second, their idea of God is totally unbiblical and unfounded. They try to put God into a mold of what they think He should be like, and therefore replace His righteousness with their own. If anything happens that they cannot understand, they may claim that God had nothing to do with it.

Let me ask you a question: If God is not in control, then who is? If no one or nothing is in control, doesn't everything happen as the result of chance or luck? Even Christians throw around the ideas of *luck* and *good fortune.* When I hear this, I immediately know that they do not understand God's Word. Scripture is clear: God is not in the luck business; He is in the blessing business.

If we replace God's sovereignty with sheer luck, we are simply saying that there is no plan or order in the universe, and we are the victims of our circumstances. If that is the case, then sometimes we'll be happy, most of the time we'll be unfulfilled, and we will always fear the future.

God does not want us to live like this. He is in absolute control of every single event in this life. He is the Master over the things that affect His purpose for each of us. How can we be sure? Let's open God's Word and examine some passages that reveal His sovereignty. First, let me say that we will not find a passage in the Bible in which God exclaims, "Thus saith the Lord God, 'I am sovereign!'" Rather than just using words, God uses life itself to reveal His absolute control.

Because God uses life to demonstrate His sovereignty, it is natural to begin our look at the biblical evidence in the very first word of Scripture, GENESIS 1:1, "In the beginning God created the heavens and the earth." Think about what this means: God created everything that exists out of nothing. He put this and every other world in its place and created galaxies, solar systems, gravity, time, space . . . literally every speck of matter in the universe. If He set all of this in motion, then He is more than able to sustain His creation for eternity.

The Old Testament reveals God's control in every area; most notably, His control of nature, nations, and even unbelievers. For example, His dominion over nature is noted in PSALM 135:6–7, which explains,

Whatever the LORD pleases, He does,

In heaven and in earth, in the seas and in all deeps.

He causes the vapors to ascend from the ends of the earth;

Who makes lightnings for the rain,

Who brings forth the wind from His treasuries.

PSALM 104:14 further illustrates this point: "He causes the grass to grow for the cattle, and vegetation for the labor of man, so that he may bring forth food from the earth." This shows that despite man's involvement with farming, it would be impossible if God did not raise the vegetation from the earth. Man can do only so much; God, however, is not bound by nature.

Now, when we think about the history of the world and the many nations that have brought about pain, war, and bloodshed, it is easy to wonder whether God was in control of these events. In the face of war, isn't it easier to believe that vicious, volatile men are in charge rather than God?

We need to understand that God is not worried about world dictators because the only reason they are in positions of power is that the Lord allowed them to be. JOB 12:23 states, "He makes the nations great, then destroys them; He enlarges the nations, then leads them away." PSALM 22:28 further stresses this idea: "The kingdom is the LORD's and He rules over the nations."

No nation, president, dictator, or army does anything outside of God's control. This does not mean that we will understand why certain things happen. There are obviously some atrocities—such as the Holocaust—that seem to defy explanation. However, we have the assurance of Scripture that—even when we do not understand His plan—God remains in control of every nation.

Something else we often fail to understand is that God is sovereign over those who do not even believe in Him. How can God reign in the life of an unbeliever? DANIEL 4:28–37 tells a wonderful story about the

Babylonian king Nebuchadnezzar. In verse 30, the king reflected on his greatness, saying, "Is this not Babylon the great, which I myself have built as a royal residence by the might of my power and for the glory of my majesty?" How's that for arrogance? He praised only himself for what God had allowed him to accomplish.

God heard Nebuchadnezzar's boasts, and the Lord responded, "Nebuchadnezzar, to you it is declared: sovereignty has been removed from you" (DAN. 4:31). God went on to explain how He would humble the mighty king until he recognized "that the Most High is ruler over the realm of mankind and bestows it on whomever He wishes" (DAN. 4:32).

In verse 37, we see the king after he had undergone his humbling experience of proclaiming honor and praise to "the King of heaven." Even this unbelieving ruler of a mighty nation realized that his control came only from God.

Because we know that God is in control, we can find peace in several assurances from the Father. First, we find comfort in the fact that almighty God—who is in absolute control of everything—is intimately and continually involved in our individual lives every single day. God never stops providing for, protecting, watching over, or caring for each of us. Because He is sovereign and all-knowing, He knows exactly what we need for today and tomorrow.

Because God is sovereign, we have the assurance that He will work out every single circumstance in our lives for something good, no matter what. It may be painful, difficult, or seemingly impossible, but God can and will use that situation to achieve His divine purpose. ROMANS 8:28 makes this clear: "We know that God causes all things to work together for good to those who love God, to those who are called according to His purpose." This claim makes sense only when we realize that God is in complete control.

We have the assurance that nothing can touch us apart from the permissive will of God. PSALM 34:7 explains, "The angel of the LORD encamps around those who fear Him, and rescues them." God is our Protector. When something happens that is painful or unexplainable in our lives, does that mean God lost control for a moment? No, because we know that these things cannot happen unless God allows them. This hope enables us to step boldly into the future because we know that God will be there for us, forever protecting us and guiding our steps.

My friend, when you begin to understand that God is in complete control of this world and everything in it, your life will change forever. God is sovereign. He is omniscient—He can answer your most trying questions. He is omnipotent—He is strong enough to overcome your biggest obstacle. He is omnipresent—wherever you may go, He will be there with you. No matter what pain, trial, or tragedy comes your way, rejoice that your Father will be there to work it out for your good, no matter what.

GROWING STRONGER THROUGH TRIALS

Adversity is one of life's inescapable experiences, and not one of us is ever happy when it affects us personally. A popular theology says, "Just trust God and think rightly; then you won't have hardship." In searching the Scriptures, however, we see that God has advanced His greatest servants through adversity, not prosperity.

God isn't interested in building a generation of fainthearted Christians. Instead, He uses trials to train up stalwart, spirit-filled soldiers for Jesus Christ. Most of us don't even want to hear about difficulties, let alone live them, but it is far better to learn about adversity *before* you experience it than to face a hardship and wonder, *Lord, what on earth are You doing?*

We live in a fallen world so, like it or not, sin and its consequences surround us. Hardship is a part of life; it can cause discouragement and even despair, sometimes to the point of disillusionment with Christianity.

When we encounter such difficulty, we typically consider the ordeal unfair, unbelievable, and unbearable. Our attitude is usually "It's not fair, God." But we should be asking, "God, what is Your point of view?"

If our lives were free from persecution or trials—if we had everything we wanted and no problems—what would we know about our heavenly Father? Our view of Him would be unscriptural and most likely out of balance. Without adversity, we would never understand who God is or what He is like. How can God prove His faithfulness unless He allows some situations from which He must rescue us?

Do you want the kind of faith that is based *only* on what you have heard or read? It is never *your* truth until God works it into your life. Most of us memorized these words before we even understood their meaning: "Yea, though I walk through the valley of the shadow of death, I will fear no evil: for thou art with me" (PS. 23:4 KJV). But the Twenty-third Psalm didn't become a living reality until we found ourselves in the valley.

Adversity can be a deadly discouragement or God's greatest tool for advancing spiritual growth. Your response can make all the difference. Remember that God has a purpose for the hardship He's allowed, and it fits with His wonderful plan for your life.

ADVANCING THROUGH ADVERSITY

When it comes to adversity, no one is immune. All of us have experienced the heartache, pressure, and anguish caused by hardships. Whatever form our trials may take—whether sickness, financial problems, animosity, rejection, bitterness, or anger—we tend to consider them setbacks. God, however, has a different perspective. He views adversity as a way not to hinder the saints, but to advance their spiritual growth.

When facing tribulation, we often wonder where it came from: *Is this my own doing? Is this from Satan? Or is this from You, Lord?* Regardless of the specific source, ultimately all adversity that touches a believer's life must first be sifted through the permissive will of God. That is not to say everything coming your way is the Lord's will. But God *allows* everything that occurs because He sees how even adversity will fit into His wonderful purpose for your life.

According to ISAIAH 55:8–9, God's thoughts are higher than ours, so we cannot expect to understand all that He is doing. He often takes the most painful experiences of adversity and uses them to prepare us for what lies ahead. God wants us to regard our struggles the way He does so that we won't be disillusioned. Therefore, far more important than determining the source of our adversity is learning how to respond properly.

Consider Joseph, one of the very few people in the Bible about whom nothing negative is written, but whose early life is characterized by adversity. Scripture says that God was prospering Joseph in the midst of his affliction—even in a foreign jail! Every trial was part of God's equipping Joseph to become the savior of Egypt and also the savior of his own family, who would later journey there to avoid starvation.

The Bible reveals a number of reasons that the Lord allows difficulties in our lives. As we begin to comprehend His purposes, we can learn to react in ways that will strengthen rather than discourage us.

ONE OF GOD'S PRIMARY PURPOSES FOR ADVERSITY IS TO GET OUR ATTENTION

He knows when we are frozen in anger and bitterness or set on doing something our own way. He may allow adversity to sweep us off our feet. When we stand before God, stripped of our pride and self-reliance, He has our complete attention.

Saul of Tarsus, later known as the apostle Paul, had to learn a lesson this way. Proud and egotistical, he was doing everything he could to rid this earth of Christians. Then God struck him blind. Lying on the Damascus

Road, Saul asked, "Who are You, Lord?" (ACTS 9:5). God had totally captured his attention. At the time, it must have seemed like a screeching halt to his life's work; in actuality, it was the beginning of an extraordinary preaching career.

ANOTHER WAY GOD USES ADVERSITY IS TO REMIND US OF HIS GREAT LOVE FOR US

Let me ask you: If you moved out of God's will into sin, and He just let you have your way, would that be an expression of love? Of course not. He loves us too much to let us get by with disobedience.

The Bible realistically agrees that "no discipline is enjoyable while it is happening—it is painful!" (HEB. 12:11 NLT). We can all say "Amen!" to that. Just as we lovingly discipline our children to protect them from developing harmful patterns in thinking and behavior, so our heavenly Father trains us by discipline in order to bring about "a quiet harvest of right living" (HEB. 12:11 NLT).

The writer of Hebrews said, "My child, don't ignore it when the Lord disciplines you, and don't be discouraged when he corrects you. For the Lord disciplines those he loves, and he punishes those he accepts as his children" (12:5–6 NLT). So if you are experiencing adversity, allow it to be a reminder of God's great love for you.

A THIRD REASON GOD SENDS ADVERSITY IS FOR SELF-EXAMINATION

When God allowed Satan to buffet Paul with a thorn in the flesh (2 COR. 12:7), the apostle prayed three times for its removal. In the process, Paul certainly must have searched his heart, asking the Lord, "Is there sin in my life? Is my attitude right?" When we encounter adversity, we would also do well to ask, *Am I in God's will, doing what He wants me to do?*

Perhaps you've done that and confessed any known sin, but the adversity persists. God deals not only with acts of transgression, but also with preprogrammed attitudes from youth. For many believers, it isn't a matter of overt sin or not loving the Lord, but something from the past that may be stunting spiritual growth.

To deal with core issues like self-esteem, attitudes toward others, and even misguided opinions about God's capabilities, the Lord sends adversity intense enough to cause deeper examination than usual. He wants us to ask: *What fears, frustrations, and suffering from childhood are still affecting or driving me? Is an old attitude or grudge hurting me? Did a comment cause feelings of rejection or worthlessness?* An issue lying dormant for years may be hindering progress. Recognize in your adversity God's loving desire to help you reach your full spiritual potential.

A FOURTH PURPOSE FOR ADVERSITY IS TO TEACH US TO HATE EVIL AS HE DOES

Satan sells his sin program by promising pleasure, freedom, and fulfillment, but he doesn't tell you about the hidden costs. The truth is, "Whatever a man sows, this he will also reap" (GAL. 6:7).

People once trapped by drugs, alcohol, or sexual indulgence but now freed by God, will speak of their hatred for the sin. Because of the suffering, helplessness, and hopelessness they experienced, they have learned to despise the very thing they at one time desired. David agreed: "Before I was afflicted I went astray" (PS. 119:67). If we could learn to anticipate sin's ongoing and future consequences, our lives would be far holier and healthier.

If you are a parent, you need to be honest with your children about failures. There is no such thing as a perfect father or mother, and pretending to have no faults is detrimental. Our children need to understand that God allows adversity for their protection. We should be frank about our weaknesses and clearly explain sin's effect, Satan's desires, and God's solution. Warn them by explaining how you responded to sin in your life and how they can avoid it in theirs. Your children will be blessed by your honesty.

A FIFTH REASON GOD SENDS ADVERSITY IS TO CAUSE US TO REEVALUATE OUR PRIORITIES

We can become workaholics, exhausting ourselves and ignoring our children until it's too late. Or we can become so enamored of material things that we neglect the spiritual. So what happens? The Lord will do away with whatever dislocates our priorities.

God doesn't initiate family trials, but when He sees us neglecting His precious gifts or focusing in the wrong place, He may send a "breeze" of adversity as a reminder to check priorities. If the warning goes unheeded, however, a hurricane may be in the forecast. Then if we persist in ignoring the intensifying storm, it's as though He withdraws His hand and lets the adversity run its full course.

For example, many fathers and mothers work hard to balance career and parenthood. There are inevitable points of conflict between the two, which can serve as cautionary breezes. But if priorities are misaligned, and moving up the corporate ladder becomes the exclusive goal, a whirlwind of adversity may be approaching.

ANOTHER IMPORTANT PURPOSE FOR ADVERSITY IS TO TEST OUR WORKS

God already knew the outcome when He told Abraham to sacrifice his son. His purpose was not to discover what the response would be, but to show the patriarch where he was in his obedient walk of faith. When Abraham came off that mountain, not only did he know more about God than ever before; he also understood more about himself spiritually.

Besides that, Isaac more than likely never forgot the experience! Children often remember things we do not expect—things far deeper than the externals. More than the sight of that pointed dagger, Isaac likely remembered that he had a father whose obedience to God knew no boundaries.

So when God sends adversity to test us, do our family members watch us buckle, or do they see us standing strong in faith, trusting the Lord to teach us, strengthen us, and bring good from the circumstance? Remember that our response carries a weighty influence for good or for evil in the lives of those who love us most.

As you face hardship, keep in mind that its intensity will not exceed your capacity to bear it. God *never* sends adversity into your life to break your spirit or destroy you. If you respond improperly, you can destroy yourself, but God's purpose is always to bless, to strengthen, to encourage, and to bring you to the maximum of your potential.

Adversity touches every life. Instead of running from it, ask the Lord, "What are You trying to teach me?" While it's okay to tell Him you don't like it and you wish He'd take it away, I challenge you to add, "But don't quit, God, until You have finished."

FINDING TRUE PEACE IN ALL CIRCUMSTANCES

Sometimes the trials aren't the tsunamis that threaten to destroy us. Instead they pour on us like a steady rain that won't stop until we have had enough. When I am shouldering a particularly stressful load at work, I find that small things bring to the surface the heavier weight I am carrying. Often it happens on Fridays when I'm trying to wrap up the week's work and prepare for a sermon. The workday begins innocently enough and then the telephone rings. The person on the other end asks for information I do not have at that moment, but I promise to have it within the hour. I hang up the phone, feeling confident that the one interruption will not change my outlook on the day.

A few minutes later, the phone rings again. There is a meeting that shouldn't be rescheduled—it will only take fifteen minutes. I rush off to that meeting and return an hour later, realizing that I have failed to keep my promise to the earlier request and am in jeopardy of missing another important deadline. I begin to restructure my day, wondering how I will accomplish everything I need to. The pace quickens and the pressure builds.

I think everyone can relate to this scenario. Whether you work in a corporate setting or shuttle your children from home to school to soccer practice to music lessons and back home again, you know the weight of responsibility and its effect on your outlook. Corporate employees are not the only ones who deal with the changing climate of our demanding world. Full-time moms know all too well what it feels like to face intense pressure. I have heard many dads say they would gladly change places with their wives—until they were left alone with their children for a weekend.

We all face stress. The death of a loved one, an accident on the way home from the grocery store, or the loss of one's home to storm damage can leave us struggling with feelings of hopelessness, doubt, and confusion. But God has a solution for our tensions and pressures. He knows our longing for peace and safety, and He has promised to provide both for us.

THE GREATEST NEED

Before His arrest, Jesus told His disciples, "Peace I leave with you; My peace I give to you; not as the world gives do I give to you. Do not let your heart be troubled, nor let it be fearful" (JOHN 14:27). Jesus knew the days following His arrest and crucifixion would be unlike anything the disciples had experienced. Stress, panic, disbelief, and anxiety would converge on them. Jesus knew the peace of God was the one thing that would stabilize the hearts and minds of His disciples after He died.

At times, our world is very chaotic. However, nothing we encounter is beyond God's reach. No problem is too great for Him to solve. No stress is too much for Him to handle. Jesus understands what it feels like to be under pressure. While He was on earth, the Lord faced many a trial and triumphed over every one. Wherever He went, people gathered, reaching out to touch Him in hopes of being healed. They hungrily clung to every word He said. Luke wrote, "Now it happened that while the crowd was pressing around [Jesus] and listening to the word of God, He was standing by the lake of Gennesaret; and He saw two boats lying at the edge of the lake . . . He got into one of the boats, which was Simon's, and asked him to put out a little way from the land" (LUKE 5:1–3). Because the people were pressing against Him, the Lord stepped into Simon Peter's boat and instructed Peter to move away from the shoreline. He adjusted to the pressure so that He could continue to be effective in His delivery of God's Word.

We may have to adjust to the pressures that God allows to come our way. But there will never be a time when He fails to provide a path through the difficulty. His peace is a gift, and it is available in all circumstances.

PEACE THROUGH PRAYER

One of the ways Jesus dealt with the pressures of life was by stepping away from the furious pace of His world to be alone with the Father. He understood that communion with God was essential to maintaining His relationship with the Father. It also is essential to experiencing peace on a continuous basis.

When we go to God in prayer, we express our needs and total dependence on Him. The psalmist wrote, "Cast your burden upon the LORD and He will sustain you; He will never allow the righteous to be shaken" (PS. 55:22). The idea of casting or rolling our burden onto the Lord is that we acknowledge Him as our sufficiency. He is our Burden Bearer, and He can carry the weight that accompanies a stressful situation.

Many people struggle in prayer because they feel guilt over past sin. They think that because they have sinned against God in the past, He won't hear their prayers. God wants us to know that He is waiting for us to come to Him, just as the father waited for the prodigal son (LUKE 15:20).

When we go to God in prayer, we find that He receives us with unconditional love and forgiveness. Never hesitate to take your problems to God in prayer. He knows your need for peace even before you ask.

FIND A QUIET PLACE

After particularly intense times of ministering to people, Jesus said to His disciples: "Come away by yourselves to a secluded place and rest a while" (MARK 6:31). When stress builds and there is no relief in sight, we need to take Jesus' advice and find a quiet place to be alone with God in prayer. I have a prayer closet at work and at home. Without spending time alone with the Father, there is no way that I could continue to do the work God has called me to do. My quiet, intimate time with Him is the one thing, above all else, that has buoyed me up for more than seven decades of life's hardest challenges. If there is one thing I exhort you to do, it is to spend time alone with the Lord every day.

Too much stress over a period of time weakens us physically, mentally, and emotionally. We need breaks even after times of rewarding activity. Jesus and the disciples had been doing what God called them to do. Yet they needed rest and renewal.

You may not be able to walk away from the pressures of life. Parents and caretakers, in particular, find it difficult to get away from the constant demands on their time. But even if you have to get up early in the morning to be alone with God, it is worth it. When I began having a quiet time with God at three o'clock in the morning, I realized that I had cut my sleep back from eight hours a night to six. Yet I had more energy than I did when I got more sleep. The Lord will reward any effort to grow closer to Him.

Wherever you are in life, you can experience God's peace deep within your soul. Peace comes when you acknowledge your love for the Lord and release your control over your situation. This does not mean you avoid responsibility; it means you acknowledge your need of God. In doing so, you can find solitude in your spirit through Jesus Christ. Turn to Him in prayer even if it is only for a few minutes every morning. When you do, you'll find that it makes a tremendous difference.

There are four essentials to experiencing the peace of God.

1. TOTAL DEPENDENCE ON THE LORD

As long as you strive and struggle to accomplish goals in your own ability, you will experience anxiety and stress. Acknowledging God as your strength and refuge shifts your focus from yourself and your finite ability to God and His infinite ability. Give God your burdens. Let Him take care of you so you can enjoy His peace.

2. PRAYER

There is a saying that goes like this: "No prayer; no peace. Know prayer; know peace." Prayer and meditation on God's Word are essential to experiencing true peace. When we hide God's Word in our hearts, the storms may blow, but they will not shatter our peace. It also is in times of prayer that we learn to worship the Lord and praise Him for what He is doing in our lives. These form a cornerstone to our intimacy with Christ. Without them, it is difficult to know the full depth of God's love.

3. FAITH

The absence of faith leads to anxiety, which is the antithesis of peace. "Shalom," God's sweet peace, does not depend on our external circumstances. It depends only on God. Before His arrest and crucifixion, Jesus reminded His followers that they would have trouble in this world, but that He would be with them always, even to the end of the age (JOHN 16:33). Residing in peace is something you can experience to its fullest because God has promised never to leave or forsake you (HEB. 13:5). Even in times of your personal failure, God's love is directed toward you. Childlike faith is all that He requires.

4. FOCUS ON GOD

Dependence, prayer, and faith must have an object. If your eyes are focused on the problem, anxiety will capture your emotions. However, if you are focused on God, then you can rest in the fact that He will give you the wisdom, strength, and especially the peace you need to complete the task or to withstand the pressure.

God has something for us to learn through each trial. He never wastes our sorrows. He uses each one to draw us closer to Him. In 2 Corinthians, the apostle Paul wrote, "We are afflicted in every way, but not crushed; perplexed, but not despairing; persecuted, but not forsaken; struck down, but not destroyed" (4:8–9). True peace does not come as a result of eliminating sorrows and disappointments. It comes as a result of one thing, and that is an intimate relationship with the Lord Jesus Christ. He is where anxiety ends and peace begins.

SUGGESTED BIBLE READING

MALACHI 3:3; PSALMS 22:28; 23; 34:7; 55:22;
103:19–22; 104; 119:67; 135:6–7; JOB 12:23;
DANIEL 4:28–37; ROMANS 8:28; ISAIAH 55:8–9;
ACTS 9:5; HEBREWS 12:5–11; 13:5; COLOSSIANS
12:7; GALATIANS 6:7; JOHN 14:27; LUKE 5:1–3;
15:20; MARK 6:31; and 2 CORINTHIANS 4:8–9.

PRAYER

Dear heavenly Father, thank You for the hardships that
You bring into my life. Please teach me through them,
and show me how to accept them as Your work in my
life. Amen.

JOURNAL QUESTIONS

- Is God refining you by fire in any area of your life?

_____

_____

_____

- If so, list the things you have not released to Him.

_____

_____

_____

- When you reach a point of forgiveness (where someone else is involved), go to the appropriate people and tell them of your forgiveness.

_____

_____

_____

- Do you require forgiveness from another party? If so, go to that person, admit your fault, and ask for forgiveness.

_____

_____

_____

Even when the world seems to turn upside down, God is in complete control. Learn more about His sovereignty and His purpose for adversity at _www.InTouch.org_.

PRINCIPLE
8

FIGHT YOUR BATTLES ON YOUR KNEES, AND YOU'LL WIN EVERY TIME

If I asked whether or not you knew how to pray, you would probably answer, "Sure I do! All Christians know how to pray!" However, if you seriously examined the track record of your answered prayers, you might not be so sure.

In MATTHEW 7:7–11, Jesus emphasized an important principle about prayer. Dispelling the assumption that prayer simply "comes naturally" for Christians, He asserted that prayer is an intentional, learned activity for God's children. In this passage, the Lord was quite simply showing the disciples the three basic steps for an effective prayer life: ask, seek, and knock.

Unfortunately well-meaning Christians can miss fantastic opportunities and blessings because they have taken a completely passive role in their prayer lives. Too often, seeking and knocking are overlooked as the believer merely asks God for something once or twice and then sits back and forgets all about the matter.

For example, when a high school student begins to make college plans, what would happen if he simply sat on the couch and said, "Lord, please show me exactly where You want me to go to college"? Now, on the surface, this seems to be the best way to start the process. But what if the young man never gets off the couch? Instead of talking with other students, visiting campuses, ordering catalogs, reviewing school Web sites, and meeting with counselors, the boy simply sits and waits for an answer from the Lord. Most likely he would still be sitting there when classes started the next fall!

Or think about someone who honestly desires a deeper understanding of Scripture, sets his Bible down on the table, and prays, "Lord, please open up the truths of the Scriptures to me. I desperately want to understand Your Word." That person can pray continuously, but the only way for him to get a deeper understanding of the Bible would be not simply to ask, but also to seek by digging into the Word of God. Even that is not enough! He would have to knock on the doors of some Scriptures, dealing with difficult passages in order to see them open up in their fullness.

What about matters of spiritual warfare? How should a Christian pray when he is under attack? Do two-sentence platitudes work then? If you ever hope to defeat your spiritual enemy—and you have a very real enemy—you must begin with prayer.

LEARNING TO PRAY THE BIBLE WAY

When you pray, do you have confidence that God will answer, or do you feel unworthy of His attention? Are your prayers specific or general? Is your prayer life a haphazard response to needs and desires, or nourishment for the life of the Lord Jesus Christ within you? One of the simplest but most profound passages on prayer in all of the Bible is found in the Sermon on the Mount:

Ask, and it will be given to you; seek, and you will find; knock, and it will be opened to you. For everyone who asks receives, and he who seeks finds, and to him who knocks it will be opened. Or what man is there among you who, when his son asks for a loaf, will give him a stone? Or if he asks for a fish, he will not give him a snake, will he? If you then, being evil, know how to give good gifts to your children, how much more will your Father who is in heaven give what is good to those who ask Him! (MATT. 7:7–11)

Prayer is not only asking and receiving, but also giving thanks to, adoring, and praising the Lord God. There are two responsibilities in prayer— God's responsibility and our responsibility. You cannot have one without the other; prayer is both divine and human. Notice the Lord's intensity in the progression in this passage: "ask . . . seek . . . knock." Clearly Jesus had in mind that we are to become actively involved in the prayer process. Prayer is not a spectator sport!

Every request, every desire of our hearts, and every need should begin with prayer—asking God for permission, seeking to know His will. Because Jesus Christ has come into our lives and because He has now *become* our Life, we have the privilege and the authority to approach Him and make a request (EPH. 3:11–12; HEB. 4:16).

God is always in the process of answering prayer. This message is the primary purpose of MATTHEW 7:7–11. Somebody may ask, "Does that mean anybody and everybody can ask, seek, knock, and find?" No, because the Sermon on the Mount is addressed to the followers of Christ. He is talking about His own children.

There is a vital element in prayer that most people overlook, which is steadfastness in prayer. We may not see anything happening, but a delay between our asking and our receiving doesn't mean that God refuses to answer our prayers. In LUKE 18:1–8, Jesus told a parable of a persistent widow who bothered a judge so much that he finally gave her what she wanted. Christ used this example to teach His followers how they ought to pray, not losing heart. Why did Jesus place this emphasis on perseverance? Because He very often delays answering prayer requests, even if your request is, in fact, the will of God. Why does God delay? If He sees within us attitudes of rebellion, bitterness, or unforgiveness, or if He notices certain unhealthy habits in our lifestyles, God postpones the answer for His children. He may already have it packaged and ready to send your way, but He cannot and will not do so until you are in a spiritual position to receive it.

A second reason for God's delay is that He is in the process of testing our sincerity in order to build into us a persistent spirit. If we are really earnest, we will not make our request known just once and then give up if it goes unanswered for a time. That is why God says to pray, and to keep on praying, asking, seeking, and knocking. Persevere. Don't give up. Endure. Hang in there—even when you do not see any evidence that God will answer your prayer in the way you hope He will.

Third, God often delays answering prayer in order to build our faith. He strengthens our trust by testing us. How does God test us? Sometimes by withdrawing. As you and I begin to ask, seek, and knock, something happens in our walk with God. When we talk to Him, we are building and nourishing our relationship with Him. We are getting to know Him— who He is and how He operates. Do you realize that once you have become one of His children, what God wants to give you above everything else is Himself? He wants you to know Him.

A fourth reason for God's delays is to develop patience within us as we endure in prayer until His timing is right. God's timing does not always match our own. He is far more interested in our knowing Him than our getting from Him everything our hearts desire.

Would you say that prayer is a vital part of your daily schedule? There is no way for Jesus Christ to be a part of my life unless I am a praying man. I talk, share, and relate with Him all day long. He is my Life! I can tell you every moment I spend with Him is a blessing.

I know countless Christians who become involved in so many activities that prayer begins to shift aside as they diligently go about serving the Lord in their own strength and wisdom. One of the primary reasons we do not pray is that we have busied ourselves with so many distractions that we don't have time for the truly important things. Why do we do this? I'm convinced it's a matter of denial and avoidance. We're not willing for God to take His scalpel, open us up all the way down to our innermost beings, and deal with things that we have never overcome.

Do you realize that one of the largest veins of gold ever discovered in America was found only three feet from where previous miners had stopped digging? Christians often experience the same problem; just beyond where we quit, just out of reach from where we are willing to go, is God's greatest blessing.

If you petition God and He shows you clearly that it is not His will, then naturally you should stop praying about it. However, if there is something that you believe God is working out in your life, or if there is a serious, deep-felt need, do not stop praying. God wants to answer that prayer. I can think of times when everything in me wanted to stop, and I would just keep on praying and crying out to God. Sure enough, suddenly, with no warning, the veil would lift; and there would be the answer, staring me right in the face. If I had quit the day before, I would have made some foolish decision on my own and missed what God wanted to provide.

Nowhere does the Bible say that prayer is easy. It involves a struggle—there will be times when Satan will attack you as you are on your knees, harassing you with doubt and sending distracting thoughts into your mind. One of Satan's most effective weapons is to cause you to have feelings of worthlessness before God. I am speaking not of proper humility, but of an unhealthy sense of unworthiness. Scripture shatters this fear by boldly proclaiming that you and I have freedom in Christ to approach the very throne of God in prayer. When you go to the Lord, do not be meek and embarrassed; instead, bow before Him and rejoice! Exclaim, "Lord

Jesus, I praise Your name that You are my Life. I thank You that I can come to You in confidence because You have told me to ask, seek, and knock. Lord, I'm coming as Your child, confident that You are listening to what I am saying. Certain that You will give me direction for my life. Confident that You are going to answer my prayer. I praise You and I accept ahead of time the answers for my prayer. Praise God. Amen!"

We do not always like the answers that God gives. He did not promise to give us anything we request; instead, He promises in MATTHEW 7:11 that everything He gives is good for us. Surely you would not want God to give you something that would harm you or ultimately destroy your life, would you? For that reason, Jesus sets the limitation up front; He says that He will give us only what is good.

Do not worry about asking God for something too big. You cannot ask God for anything so monumental that He cannot do it if He deems it to be good. God is honored by large, difficult, and impossible requests when we ask, seek, knock, and trust our loving Father always to answer for our good.

If you will actively apply this simple truth, God will transform your prayer life, which will in turn transform your relationships, effectiveness, family, business, and all other aspects of your life. The privilege of prayer is a heritage that belongs to every child of God, a potential that is beyond human understanding. It is a work of God's grace that He has given to each one of us. It is my prayer that you will not let that heritage be wasted in your life. Allow God to make you the man, woman, or young person that He desires you to be. Learn to relate to Him. Nourish that inner being of Christ in your prayer life. Make your daily prayer life an ongoing, intimate relationship of conversation with the Lord Jesus Christ.

Once you establish a prayer life with God, you will begin to harness His strength to fight your spiritual battles. When you fight your battles on your knees, you'll win every time!

A REAL ENEMY

We hear about conflicts and attacks taking place all over the world, but they often seem very distant. The truth is that every single one of us faces a war each day—we battle the devil. Yet many people do not recognize the work of Satan; they mistake his assault for the struggles of everyday life.

An enemy always wants to be camouflaged and covered so he can walk in the shadows undetected. Satan loves for people to doubt his existence, but do not be deceived—he is very real. Jesus clearly recognized the reality of the devil, who tempted Him in the wilderness (MATT. 4:1). And we know Paul believed the scriptural account of Satan's temptation in the Garden (GEN. 3) because in 2 CORINTHIANS 11:3, he referred to the serpent that deceived Eve.

Satan is a liar. He tries to convince us that he does not exist. He wants us to believe that all religions are the same and everybody will get to heaven by one way or another. That is the way he operates: it all sounds good, but it is a lie.

Our enemy is very deliberate in the way he approaches us. He appeals to our minds first. We do not immediately act according to our temptations. The downward spiral begins with our thoughts. Our bodies simply turn in the direction our minds are facing.

We read in 2 CORINTHIANS 10:5: "We are destroying speculations and every lofty thing raised up against the knowledge of God, and we are taking every thought captive to the obedience of Christ." We must deliberately take control of our thinking because the mind is the battleground where Satan confronts us. If we are to win the battle against Satan, we must bring our thoughts under the control of the Lord Jesus Christ.

Satan is a formidable foe. We may be able to control some of our thoughts, but we cannot resist him on our own. Left to our natural devices, we will sin by saying, "It's okay. Everybody does it. That does not apply to our culture—the Bible is outdated." Such thinking stems from allowing the devil entrance into our minds. We must actively guard our thinking against his deceitfulness.

The battle for our salvation was won at the cross—the devil knows he is a defeated foe, destined for eternity in hell. Since he cannot take a single child of God with him, he tries to destroy our witness instead. However, when we recognize Satan's deception and depend upon the strength of Jesus Christ to resist him, we can be confident of victory.

THE STRENGTH TO STAND

Have you ever faced circumstances so overwhelming that you wondered how you would stand up under them? At times, we all have feelings of weakness. Though none of us enjoy those experiences, periods of powerlessness and vulnerability are not necessarily negative. If our weakness results in self-pity, despair, or sin, then it is harmful, but if it drives us to dependency upon God, it is beneficial. Oftentimes fear and discouragement are caused by satanic attack—a willful, determined assault by the devil for the purpose of harming your spirit, soul, or body.

Satan is not omnipotent, but he is nonetheless a very powerful adversary. God does not leave us to fend for ourselves, however, and He wants us to understand the fullness and certainty of His supernatural capacity to help us. That is why EPHESIANS 6:10 tells us to be strong in the Lord and the power of His might. When you trust Jesus as your Savior, the Holy Spirit comes to indwell in you. Living inside you is a member of the Trinity who has supernatural power—power greater than Satan's—to enable you to stand firm. The same divine power that created the heavens and earth, calmed the ocean, and raised the dead is available to every believer through the Lord Jesus Christ and is absolutely essential during spiritual attacks.

The Bible tells us to stand firm and resist the devil (EPH. 6:11; JAMES 4:7). It does not say, "Arm yourself and go fight him," for the simple reason that the battle for our salvation has already been won at the cross.

Once you are God's child, you are eternally secure—Satan cannot have your soul, or your eternal life (JOHN 10:29–30). But his goal is to thwart the Lord's plan for you, and he can do a significant amount of damage. He is out to steal your peace and joy, cause confusion and anger, and encourage wrong relationships in your life. He will do anything he can to cheat you out of the blessings the Lord has promised. And the holier you attempt to live before God, the stronger the attacks are likely to be. Satan is after your testimony—he wants to ruin your witness and make you as ineffective as possible.

Would you say that yours is a holy life and that you are walking in obedience to God? If not, you may have yielded to some satanic attack, believed the devil's lie, and given yourself over to him in some way. What may have seemed like an innocent temptation at first can eventually exert a viselike grip on you. Christians are to be under God's control, but the enemy ultimately wants you under his influence, and he will do his best to destroy everything good in your life. Satan's objectives are very clear, namely, to draw believers away from God and cheat the Lord out of the glory He deserves. As long as the devil is around, we will suffer his assaults, so the question is not how to avoid satanic attacks, but how to overcome them.

Paul laid out the battle plan in the sixth chapter of Ephesians. First, we must identify the enemy (VV. 11–12); second, we are to dress in the full armor of God and stand firm (VV. 13–17). The next verse reveals the key to withstanding Satan's onslaughts—we must appropriate the strength of the living God. How do we get His power into our lives, to be unleashed in any and every circumstance? There is only one way: by prayer (V. 18).

It is through prayer that the Lord releases His energy, divine power, and protection, enabling us to live a godly, holy, and peaceful life regardless of our circumstances. It is only through prayer that our minds and spirits can discern what the average person cannot detect. Only through prayer can we sense forewarnings of Satan's attacks, which can be aimed anywhere—finances, family, relationships, or health. The one thing Satan hates above all else is the believer who knows how to persist in prayer and claim the promises of God—the enemy has no defense against persevering prayer, which crushes his might and sends him running. On the other hand, when we do not pray, we set ourselves up for defeat.

We have this power available to us, and yet we often fail to stand firmly against satanic attacks. Since our enemy knows the power of prayer, he will use distractions against us to get our minds focused on anything but prayer. He will do everything possible to keep us from spending time in communion with our heavenly Father. Satan wants us too busy to talk to the One who knows everything, loves us always, and desires to defend us in any situation.

Paul knew how essential it is to recognize prayer's role in protecting us against spiritual attack. Our heavenly Father sees the whole combat zone in which you and I live each day. He knows where we are in the battlefield and the nature of our weaknesses. He is also aware of what Satan is up to in our lives—every cunning device, exactly where he will attack, and who he will use in the effort.

If you are prayerless, if you don't cry out for His divine direction and guidance, and if you don't put on His armor by faith every day, the enemy is going to succeed. And more than likely, he will hit you where you do not expect him to because that is his battle strategy.

The importance of prayer cannot be overemphasized. Your understanding of Scripture will be in direct proportion to your prayers. The holiness and righteousness of your life are directly related to your prayers. Your fruitfulness and usefulness to almighty God are also proportional to your communication with the Father. It is critical that you understand praying is not "Lord, bless me, bless him, bless her. Give me this; give me that." Those little, quick prayers are fine if you're "prayed up." Serious praying, however, is talking to your heavenly Father, who listens and desires to answer. It is about humbling yourself and acknowledging not only your need but also His presence, His holiness, and His righteousness. The source of our strength is the living God, and His power is channeled into our lives primarily when we listen and talk with Him.

Understanding exactly what it takes to release God's awesome power, Paul wrote, "With all prayer and petition pray at all times in the Spirit" (EPH. 6:18). By "all prayer," he was referring to prayer in general, that is, requests, thanksgiving, praise, and intercession (prayer to God on behalf of others), all of which are important. Next, he used the word "petition," which speaks of a particular, singular request. God displays His power through prayer when we ask for something specific and He does exactly what we requested. But if we are praying only "Bless me, bless this, bless that," how can we know whether God has answered?

Paul also talked about praying at all times. We are most vulnerable to satanic attacks when we are not praying. Satan arranges a sequence of events in your life and mine to defeat us. He wants to get you too busy, distracted, or negligent to pray because once you are prayerless, you will soon become concerned and worried—burdens will become heavier, and you will feel discouraged and weary. Eventually you will feel emotionally, spiritually, and physically weak. Then when you drop your guard, Satan will hit you. You simply cannot afford to be prayerless!

FIRST THESSALONIANS 5:17 instructs us further with three powerful words: "Pray without ceasing." How can we pray at all times? It means living in God-consciousness. Think in terms of a telephone. If you hang up, you have disconnected the call. "Praying without ceasing" means you do not hang up—you continuously stay on the line with God. That is how He intends for us to live. If I meet somebody I have been praying for and something good has happened in his life, I will say, "Thank You, God, for what You did for him." If I see evil going on, I will say, "God, I am trusting You to correct this situation." The truth is, we should be able to talk to the Father specifically all the time. "Praying always" means living in communion with the Father, in constant awareness of His presence.

The only way we can be strong enough to withstand the traps and counterfeits of the devil is by having a relationship whereby God is always speaking to our hearts and we are always talking to Him in return. You and I cannot be discerning unless we are praying as we ought. So, when you're driving down the expressway, what are you thinking about? Why don't you talk to God? When you wash the dishes and clean your house, what are you thinking about? You can talk to the Father. Talk to Him about everything. Satan wants you to think there are times when you do not need God—since he hates it when you are on your knees, he will keep you too busy to pray.

Is your prayer life pitiful or powerful? No one else can put on your spiritual armor for you. If you want God's best in your life, get on your knees. Divine, supernatural power is available if you will cry out to God and claim it by faith. Your prayers release God's power into your life and make it possible for you to stand firm against every onslaught of the devil.

THE ARMOR OF GOD

Aggravations. Frustrations. Feelings of inadequacy. Moments of doubt and fear. Where do these emotions come from? Are they self-imposed? Or do we have another force working against us, someone who, if he could, would destroy our peace and give solid evidence to our fears?

We would be remiss to give Satan credit for everything that goes wrong in our lives. Certainly the last thing we need to do as believers is to constantly focus our spiritual eyes on the enemy and his tactics. Joshua, Jehoshaphat, Nehemiah, Esther, and Daniel had one thing in common: they refused to dwell on Satan's intervention in their lives. Each faced impossible situations, yet he or she turned to God, who subsequently brought deliverance.

Although we do have a real enemy who seeks our destruction, we are not defenseless. We have the strength given to us by Christ Himself to overcome our adversary. This is our hope: that Christ overcame the deepest, darkest, strongest evil that Satan could muster. In His death and resurrection, Christ broke the power of sin and put an end to eternal death.

Satan can tempt us to sin, but we can say no to his enticements (1 COR. 10:13). We are not pawns floundering within his grasp. We belong to the Son of God; we are His, and He is our eternal Savior. Jesus won the victory and proclaims the name of all who believe in Him before God's throne of grace. Nothing can separate us from His eternal love (ROM. 8:38–39).

On the other hand, the apostle Peter cautioned us to "be of sober spirit, be on the alert. Your adversary, the devil, prowls around like a roaring lion, seeking someone to devour. But resist him, firm in your faith" (1 PETER 5:8–9).

You may ask, "If Jesus Christ has won the victory, why are we still in the battle?" The reason is that we live according to God's timetable. He knows the exact moment of Satan's final defeat. The present victory is ours on a daily basis as we cling to Jesus Christ. However, we must claim that victory and learn to walk in the Spirit, as Christ walked while He was here on earth.

One of the principal reasons for Jesus' coming was to personally identify with us—our needs, heartaches, joys, and even failures. Though Christ never suffered defeat, He knew what it was like to be separated from the Father. On the cross, for a brief time, He was separated from God as He bore our sins. But death could not hold Him. Jesus canceled mankind's sin with His atoning blood and, in so doing, set the stage for Satan's final defeat. When we realize that God understands what we are facing and is willing to provide the strength we need, then trusting Him with even the smallest details becomes a natural part of life.

Until Christ returns, we are soldiers engaged in spiritual warfare, and we have the victory when we do battle in the power and name of the living God. Peter's words of warning to us are a signal not to turn and run, but to stand firm in our faith, trusting God and refusing to be drawn aside by the temptations and deceptions of the enemy. One of the best ways to defend against and overcome Satan's ploys is to understand your position in Christ. The book of Romans is foundational in this aspect.

The apostle Paul wrote, "For all who are being led by the Spirit of God, these are sons of God. For you have not received a spirit of slavery leading to fear again, but you have received a spirit of adoption as sons by which we cry out, 'Abba! Father!' The Spirit Himself testifies with our spirit that we are children of God, and if children, heirs also, heirs of God and fellow heirs with Christ" (ROM. 8:14–17).

Satan is an enemy to be respected and understood. Instead of submitting to God and His omnipotence, the devil rebelled and drew away one-third of heaven's forces with him. Christ's victory over Satan is total and complete. Try as he may, he can never snatch the victory out of God's almighty hand. If you are living for the Lord Jesus Christ, He will empower you to do God's will so you can find blessing and safety.

Paul told us to put on the armor of God when we battle our spiritual enemies:

> Finally, be strong in the Lord and in the strength of His might. Put on the full armor of God, so that you will be able to stand firm against the schemes of the devil. For our struggle is not against flesh and blood, but against the rulers, against the powers, against the world forces of this darkness, against the spiritual forces of wickedness in the heavenly places. Therefore, take up the full armor of God, so that you will be able to resist in the evil day, and having done everything, to stand firm.
>
> Stand firm therefore, having *girded your loins with truth,* and having put on the *breastplate of righteousness,* and having *shod your feet*

with the preparation of the gospel of peace; in addition to all, taking up the *shield of faith* with which you will be able to extinguish all the flaming arrows of the evil one. And take the *helmet of salvation,* and the *sword of the Spirit,* which is the word of God. (EPH. 6:10–17, emphasis added)

Though at times—especially in our present age—it seems we are in the midst of a horrendous physical battle, the real war is against the powers of spiritual darkness. Satan's goal has not changed over the years. The enemy knows his ultimate destiny, yet he will never give up his evil intent against the kingdom of God until Christ banishes him to the eternal lake of fire (REV. 20:10). The only way he can do damage to the kingdom of God now is by enticing God's beloved children to yield to sin, thus damaging their fellowship with the Lord.

Satan will try to discourage you by filling your mind with an array of doubt and confusion, but you do not have to believe him. The message of the gospel of Christ is given to you as a sure authority. God's Word provides all the details you need to know about Satan.

Paul also admonished us to "stand firm"—a phrase that denotes extreme faith in the One who gives us life and strength. But the enemy of faith is pride—a sure road to spiritual defeat. In the ministry, I have seen many who have fallen because of pride—they have been undone by their refusal to humble themselves before God and accept His plan for their lives. This is one reason why it is tremendously important to put on the entire armor that God has given to us. The armor keeps us mindful of who is in control of our lives and who is our Advocate before the Father (1 JOHN 2:1).

On our own, we cannot defeat or even resist the enemy. Only through the power of Jesus Christ do we have the ability to stand and claim what God has done through His Son. The victory took place at Calvary (COL. 2:13–15). However, if we demand Satan's forces to leave without using the name of Jesus Christ, we position ourselves for a prideful defeat. Pride also comes into play when we think we are in control of our lives: "God is opposed to the proud, but gives grace to the humble" (JAMES 4:6).

Make a habit of claiming the armor of God each morning before you leave your house—this is a conscious act of submitting your life to the Lord as your final authority. Acknowledging your need for Him is a sign not of weakness, but of unshakable trust. When you place your faith in Jesus Christ, heaven is on your side.

Are you standing fully clothed in His armor, or do you rise in the morning, grab a cup of coffee, and run out the door? Do you think of Jesus throughout the day, hoping to make more time for Him in the evening, only to find other commitments taking His place?

Establish and commit yourself to time alone with God. Let the life of Jesus Christ be your example. Even before His day began—which was much busier than ours—Christ rose to be alone with the Father. Your life may be stretched to the limit. God knows what you are facing, and He will help you make time to be with Him if that is truly your heart's desire.

Whatever transpires in your life, the wisest decision you will ever make is the decision to spend time with the Lord on a regular basis. This teaches you to recognize Satan's movement and prepares you for battle when the enemy approaches. Paul told the Ephesians they were in a war, but clothed in the armor of God, they were assured of victory.

SUGGESTED BIBLE READING

MATTHEW 4:11; 7:7–11; EPHESIANS 3:11–12;
6:10–18; HEBREWS 4:16; LUKE 18:1–8;
2 CORINTHIANS 11:3; 1 CORINTHIANS 10:5–13;
JAMES 4:7; JOHN 10:29–30; 1 THESSALONIANS 5:17;
ROMANS 8:14–17, 38–39; 1 PETER 5:8–9;
REVELATION 20:10; 1 JOHN 2:1; COLOSSIANS
2:13–15; and JAMES 4:6.

PRAYER

Dear heavenly Father, as I begin this day, I put on, in
faith, the belt of truth—I ask You to guide me through
the decisions of my day. I put on the breastplate of
righteousness—guard my emotions and my heart, and
cause me to be pure. I put on my spiritual boots and
ask for courage to share the gospel with any who need
to hear. I put on my helmet of salvation, asking You to
bring to my mind all You have done for me through
Your Son, Jesus Christ. Finally I pick up my sword of
the Spirit and ask You to bring to my mind Scripture
that I have read, helping me to apply it to my life. I
want to bring glory to Your name. Amen.

JOURNAL QUESTIONS

- What is the armor of God?

_____

_____

_____

_____

- As you begin each day, practice putting on the armor of God.

- What is your first response to a troublesome or tempting situation?

_____

_____

_____

_____

- Who should you turn to first when trials arise? Why?

_____

_____

_____

_____

The armor of God is a serious, vital part of Scripture, yet it is often taken for granted by believers. Take an in-depth look at this and other aspects of spiritual warfare at _www.InTouch.org._

PRINCIPLE
9

THE BIBLE IS THE
SOURCEBOOK OF LIFE

In a recent survey, 60 percent of the Christians polled said they believe the Bible is "totally accurate in all of its teaching."[1] With the remaining 40 percent questioning the authority of God's Word, is it any wonder that so many Christians struggle to understand, let alone defend, their faith?

Our belief system governs our lifestyle and choices—it is the foundation from which we form our opinions and make decisions. For Christians, it is absolutely essential to know what we believe and why. Most people inherit their convictions from their parents and simply absorb those ideas without really investigating them. For instance, if their fathers supported the union, then they support the union; if their mothers voted Republican, then they vote Republican; and so on.

But to be certain our system of thinking is accurate, we must base it on the Word of God and not on habit, culture, or even family heritage. A belief system is like a mental grid through which all outside information must pass. If our mental grid has been built on the truth of the Bible, then we can detect false doctrine and philosophy.

False doctrine is usually mixed up with just enough truth to make it sound good. Many Christians who are not grounded in their faith are easily led astray by doctrines that are genuinely too good to be true. They eagerly support an agenda that is inconsistent with God's Word because it offers license to live according to one's fleshly desires (2 TIM. 4:3).

Christians should know their convictions so that they can present those beliefs convincingly to others. While it is the work of the Holy Spirit to bring the lost to Christ, God may choose to use us to instruct unbelievers in the way of truth. Our world is full of people who are desperate, lonely, and hurting. They yearn for the amazing hope that we have. But they desire hope sourced in truth, not on someone else's opinion.

There is no question that our society is permeated with godless ideas and philosophies that can ultimately destroy us. But if our belief system is based upon the Scriptures, we will recognize deceitful teaching when we hear it and will address real needs with real answers.

THE FOUNDATION FOR WHAT YOU BELIEVE

People often have difficulty expressing what they believe. Instead of having a verifiable belief system based on godly principles, too many Christians embrace a few vague ideas. Peter told us always to be ready to give a reason for what we believe (1 PETER 3:15). So we want to be sure that we correctly understand scriptural truth. Let's consider a list of absolute truths that should be a foundational part of your belief system.

THE BIBLE

The Bible is God's unfolding revelation of Himself. It is His Word to the human race, explaining His intervention in history and nature, and His arrival in this world as the God-man. In keeping with 2 TIMOTHY

3:16, we refer to the Scriptures as the inspired Word of God, or as "God-breathed," which means the Lord chose individuals to record what He spoke to them. Since He who gave the Word is more than capable of protecting it from error, the Bible we have today is as reliable as when it was originally recorded. Each new discovery of forgotten scrolls and Scripture fragments affirms the accuracy and reliability of the Bible—it has never been contradicted.

The Word of the living God was given to us so that we might grow in our relationship to Him. This is our instruction book for life and the final authority for what we believe.

THE GODHEAD

Although the specific term *Trinity* is not found in Scripture, the truth of the triune God appears throughout the Bible. Our one God consists of three distinct persons: God the Father, God the Son, and God the Holy Spirit. They are characterized by the same attributes—they are eternal, omnipotent, omniscient, omnipresent, and immutable—but each person has a different function.

Many passages of Scripture reveal a three-part Godhead. For example, the Spirit of God hovered over the waters in GENESIS 1:2, and later God said, "Let Us make man in Our image" (V. 26). Who is "Us" if not the Trinity? It is certainly not angels, because they are not creators.

Jesus likewise indicated three persons comprise the Godhead: "I will ask the Father, and He will give you another Helper, that He may be with you forever; that is the Spirit of truth" (JOHN 14:16–17). Later He admonished His disciples to baptize in the name of the Father, the Son, and the Holy Spirit (MATT. 28:19).

Our heavenly Father is the eternal and absolutely holy Creator God. He has control over every single thing, which is why the apostle Paul said He "causes all things to work together for good to those who love God, to those who are called according to His purpose" (ROM. 8:28). He must be overseeing and executing circumstances in order to make them turn out for our good.

God the Son is Jesus Christ, who took upon Himself human flesh and walked among men. Jesus never questioned His divinity, instead affirming that "He who has seen Me has seen the Father" (JOHN 14:9). He came to earth for the specific purpose of dying on the cross—His death was the substitutionary payment in full for our sin-debt (1 PETER 3:18). God the Father cannot look upon sin (PS. 66:18); consequently only a perfect, holy sacrifice could atone for it before Him. Today God the Son sits at the right hand of God the Father and makes intercession for us.

God the Holy Spirit dwells within every believer from the moment of salvation. Through Him, we have our spiritual gift(s) and the empowerment to do the work God chooses for our lives. The Holy Spirit transforms the life of the believer and brings forth good things (GAL. 5:22–23).

SATAN

The Bible tells us that God created Satan and made him an important angel (EZEK. 28:12–15). He is real. The devil so desired to be like God that he rebelled against the Creator, who subsequently cast him and his coconspirators to earth. Here he has chosen to set up a counterfeit kingdom so that he may reign as the god of this world (2 COR. 4:4). Satan uses deception and division to deceive believers; he also desires to keep unbelievers away from the saving grace of Jesus Christ, thereby destroying them. As the source of all sin, he instigates pain, sorrow, and spiritual death, but he disguises his intentions—he tries to lure people into his counterfeit kingdom by whispering to them about indulgence and doing what feels good now. Satan speaks only of the present, not the future. He never mentions consequences.

As Christians, we have no cause to fear Satan. This is true for two reasons. First, "greater is He who is in you than he who is in the world" (1 JOHN 4:4). We are under the protection of the Holy Spirit; nothing can happen to us that God does not allow, and we know that He permits only those circumstances—no matter how bad they seem—that He can turn for our good. Second, all of us who have read Scripture have seen Satan's obituary. It is in REVELATION 20 where he is thrown into a lake of fire, eternally punished for his rebellion toward almighty God (V. 10).

MAN

God created man in His image in order to love us and fellowship with us. We are also privileged to glorify and serve Him. But when Adam and Eve disobeyed God, man's relationship to the Creator changed. At the same time, man's very nature became corrupt so that each of us is born with our will inclined away from God. Consequently we are separated from our holy, perfect heavenly Father. But God provided for man's sin with His redemptive plan—the sacrifice of His Son.

No man can earn God's forgiveness or acceptance. It is a lie of Satan that any of us can substitute good works for the grace of Christ. Whatever "goodness" we have and whatever works we perform, they amount to nothing more than "filthy rags," in terms of meriting salvation (ISA. 64:6 NIV). But redemption works in our lives to change our nature and bend it back toward God.

SALVATION

The simplest definition of *salvation* is "the gift of God's grace, whereby He provides forgiveness for our sins." Throughout the Old Testament, God's faithful people brought animal sacrifices to His altar in order to atone for their sins. These blood offerings foreshadowed the once-and-for-all sacrifice that was to come. Jesus Christ, whom John the Baptist rightly called the Lamb of God, died on a cross as a substitute for us. That is, at the time of the Savior's death, God the Father placed all the sin of mankind upon Him. So our sin-debt was paid in absolute fullness. Now we are sealed in the Holy Spirit and eternally secure.

Salvation is by grace through faith in Jesus Christ; it is not something we receive based on our behavior (EPH. 2:8–9). People who are saved do good works as an extension of their changed nature. The Lord said, "I am the way, and the truth, and the life; no one comes to the Father but through Me" (JOHN 14:6). However, God gave mankind free will—we have a choice to receive the gift of grace or to reject Jesus Christ. No matter what you believe to be true about God or how good you try to be, there is no salvation for you if you reject the Son of God.

THE CHURCH

The church is the whole body of Christ—believers from every part of the globe. It has nothing to do with being Baptist, Methodist, Presbyterian, Catholic, or part of any other denomination. If you have trusted Jesus Christ as your personal Savior, you are in the body of Christ, and God is your heavenly Father. As followers of Jesus, we are to express love for one another—encouraging, helping, and praying for fellow Christians. Our conduct should be in keeping with the One we call Lord and Master of our lives.

We meet in local groups to serve the Lord. The clear work of the church is to reach out and bring people to a saving knowledge of Jesus Christ. In addition, we instruct believers so that all may grow in relationship to God. He has commanded us to "go therefore and make disciples of all the nations, baptizing them in the name of the Father and the Son and the Holy Spirit, teaching them to observe all that I commanded you" (MATT. 28:19–20).

Within the church, we practice two scriptural ordinances: baptism and the Lord's Supper. Baptism by immersion is a picture of what happens to every single person who is saved: we have put to death the old life and have risen to walk in the fullness and power of the Holy Spirit. Our character, conversation, and conduct are different because we have a new spirit—we are born again. Baptism does not save us; rather, it is an expression of obedience to Jesus' call that we be baptized in the name of the Father, the Son, and the Holy Spirit (MATT. 28:19).

Likewise, the Lord's Supper is not an optional idea, but an expression of obedience. Through the Lord's Supper, we rejoice in the blood of the new covenant between God and His children. Instead of an animal sacrifice, there is one perfect sacrifice. When we receive the elements representing Jesus' body and blood, it is a time to celebrate our forgiveness. Even more, we celebrate His resurrection and the awesome anticipation of His return.

Every one of these issues is a vital part of the Christian's belief system, and they are all found in one place—the Word of God. As His children, we own the most precious book on the face of the earth. If we know what it says, we will know what we must believe to live for His glory.

FINDING GOD'S FREQUENCY

People use all kinds of methods to make decisions. Far too many Christians choose to say, "Lord, this is what I'm going to do. If this doesn't suit You, You just let me know." Or "If this isn't Your will, You just stop me and I'll know it's not of You." That is no way to find out what God wants you to do.

Having the spiritual discernment to make wise decisions is critical. Discernment is an asset that is not acquired instantly, but grows out of a life totally consecrated to and dependent upon God. When you seek godly discernment with all your heart and your motives are pure, He will help you make wise decisions. He knows your heart, and He wants you to do the right thing.

In seeking God for perfect guidance, you must first confess your sins and allow God complete access to your mind and will. When your relationship with Jesus Christ is right, He will give you wisdom.

When you disobey God in word, action, or motive, there is a hindrance to your fellowship with the Lord, and it is difficult to receive clear guidance. When you sin, you need to confess immediately and accept the responsibility for your actions. Do not wait until you go to bed because you will live the entire day out of harmony with God. If you confess your sins, He is faithful to forgive you right then and there that the rest of the day may be right.

Are you afraid to make decisions? Do you vacillate between two paths because you can't determine which way to turn? Sometimes this is due to a self-image problem. You don't trust yourself, and you fear the consequences of making the wrong decision. Other times it is the result of sin that blocks your communication with God. How can you know what God wants you to do if your conscience is not clear?

A guilty conscience is to the mind what static is to a radio. You hear two voices that say two different things. When you struggle between your will and God's will, you don't get a clear message. There is instead a distorted, fractional sound. Your mind and will are divided, and you cannot know what God is saying.

It's time to turn the dial to God's frequency and tune in to His message for your life. When you do, He will give you the discernment and wisdom required for godly living.

THIS IS THE WAY, WALK IN IT

Have you ever had to make a decision but had no earthly idea how to go about coming to the right conclusion? Deep in your heart you really wanted to do the Lord's will, but you weren't quite sure what to do. Maybe you felt a deep need to know the mind of God. You really wanted to know what He thought. You had purposed in your spirit to do the right thing, but you just didn't know how to find what the Lord desired in that particular situation.

I believe one of the most valuable lessons that you will learn, as a

Christian, is how to acquire spiritual discernment. FIRST JOHN 5:14 declares, "This is the confidence which we have before Him, that, if we ask anything according to His will, He hears us." This is positive assurance that you can know the mind of God.

Life is composed of one decision after another. Some of them are minor decisions and some are major, but all require godly discernment. You may be facing a decision about your vocation. Maybe you feel that a change is coming or is necessary. Or you may feel the crunch of economic recession through employment insecurity. You may be asking God what you should do. Maybe you're trying to make a decision about a potential spouse. You're not sure whether it's the Lord's will for you to be married or not. Perhaps you're a student and you're trying to choose a major for your college career, and you just can't seem to get God's clear direction about it.

Whatever decision you are facing, one thing is certain: God is always willing to show you His will, His plan, and His purpose. He always desires to give you guidance and direction in your decisions. God spoke to Abraham, saying, "Abraham, get up out of the land in which you are living and go into a land that I will show you" (GEN. 12:1). He spoke to Gideon and told him to lead the people of God against those who had enslaved them (JUDGES 6:14). He sent an angel to Mary to tell her of the Christ child (LUKE 1:28-31). When Paul was headed in one direction to preach the gospel, the Holy Spirit said to him, "Paul, that's not My will for your life at this time" (ACTS 16:6–7).

Has the Lord ceased speaking to men and women today, as He did in Bible times? Absolutely not! God has spoken in many ways, recorded in the Old and the New Testaments, and He continues to speak to people today. His method of speaking may have changed, but the fact that He speaks and gives us direction for our lives has not.

The Word of God is His clear instruction as to how you should live— the basis upon which you should make decisions. God has given you the Scriptures for guidance and instruction. He has also given you the Holy

Spirit, who indwells in you to interpret the Word so that from the Word and through His Spirit, you can have assurance.

All genuine spiritual discernment comes from the Holy Spirit. It may come through another person or a Scripture reading, but the Holy Spirit makes it possible for you to hear the message as God speaks it. Here are a few practical steps that will help you listen to the Holy Spirit and acquire the spiritual discernment necessary to make wise decisions:

CLEAR THE PATHWAY OF YOUR MIND

In order to hear God's voice, you must clear your life of all known unconfessed sin. You must be willing to ask the Lord to forgive you and cleanse your life, and you must accept His shed blood on the cross as full and adequate payment for your sin. You must also clear your thinking of your personal desires. This does not mean that you empty your mind and stop thinking or having desires. But you must be willing to be neutral, so you can honestly open yourself to God's will for your life.

EXERCISE PATIENCE

One key to finding spiritual discernment is patience. You must be willing to wait until God shows you His way. Patience is a sure sign of spiritual maturity. JAMES 1:4 states, "Let endurance have its perfect result, so that you may be perfect and complete, lacking in nothing."

RESIST PRESSURE

Pressure is one of your greatest enemies when you seek to discern God's will. There are two types of pressure: external (the pressure of other people's opinions or imposed time limits) and internal (the pressure of your spirit). When you make a decision based upon perceived pressure, rather than clear guidance and direction from God, you risk doing the wrong thing.

PERSIST IN PRAYER

The key in this area is not simply praying, but persisting in prayer. That is, throughout the day—in the morning, in the afternoon, and in the evening—pray consistently and passionately (1 THESS. 5:17). Prayer is God's way of preparing you for an answer. As you begin to pray, He begins to show you things in your life, such as attitudes or motives, that need to be examined.

LEAN ON HIS PROMISES

When you face a major decision, turn to the Word of God and ask Him to show you a promise. The Scriptures are full of God's promises, which are evidence of His divine guidance. God said, "I will instruct you and teach you in the way which you should go; I will counsel you with My eye upon you" (PS. 32:8). The author of Proverbs told Christians to "trust in the LORD with all your heart and do not lean on your own understanding. In all your ways acknowledge Him, and He will make your paths straight" (3:5–6). These are specific promises that God truly desires to give you guidance and direction for your life.

WAIT FOR PEACE

COLOSSIANS 3:15 urges you to "let the peace of Christ rule in your heart." Regardless of the pressure you may feel, wait for peace. You may seek confirmation from others, but be careful that their confirmation is in keeping with what God has said in His Word. Perfect peace is God's verdict when you have His mind and His way. Don't budge until you get God's peace. This is the final confirmation of a wise decision.

Spiritual discernment is critical in every area of life, no matter how small, because every decision has an effect upon your fellowship with the Lord and the fulfillment of His will. If you don't acquire spiritual discernment, you will begin to respond from your feelings and instant reactions.

You will do what comes naturally. When a Christian does this, he is no longer doing what comes spiritually, as it is always natural for the flesh to disobey God.

That is why it is critical to discern God's will in *everything* you do. If you could get a glimpse of His genuine personal interest and involvement in your life, you would have a deeper appreciation, devotion, and sense of adoration toward God. Have you ever thought about how interested God is in your daily affairs—those little, insignificant things that don't seem to make a difference to most people?

Christians often separate the spiritual life from the common, everyday life. God never intended that to be the approach you take. He intends to be involved in every decision you make, no matter how small.

If you want to make wise decisions, you must live consecrated—you must walk committed to Him. Every morning surrender your life to Him. Separate yourself to Him, for Him, and under Him for that day. Paul said, "I urge you, brethren, by the mercies of God, to present your bodies as a living and holy sacrifice, acceptable to God, which is your spiritual service of worship. And do not be conformed to this world, but be transformed by the renewing of your mind, so that you may prove what the will of God is, that which is good and acceptable and perfect" (ROM. 12:1–2).

Every believer can walk in confidence and assurance that he is walking in God's will. If you clear your conscience, wait patiently, resist pressure, persist in prayer, lean on His promises, and wait for His peace, He will speak truth to your heart and mind. ISAIAH 30:21 states, "Your ears will hear a word behind you, 'This is the way, walk in it,' whenever you turn to the right or to the left.'"

This is a beautiful example of how the Lord speaks to our hearts. Day by day I have to ask, "Lord, what next?" And I have to hear Him say, *This is the way. Walk in it.* I hear that many times during the day. The Lord will say the same thing to you. You can't always trust counsel from other people to tell you what is the right way. If you are committed to Jesus Christ—if

He is your Savior, your Master, your Lord—and it is your heart's desire to follow Him, you will find a confidence in your spiritual life that you have never known before. If you will listen carefully, He will whisper to you very quietly, *My child, this is the way. Walk in it.*

WALK WISELY

From God's perspective we live our lives in one of two ways: wisely or unwisely. Those who learn to walk wisely in the power of God's truth have blessing and hope for the future. However, the opposite is true when unwise decisions are made. Therefore, we need to know how to make wise choices. David learned to do this by placing his trust in God. He also found that many times walking wisely required patience and his willingness to wait for God's guidance.

In the Psalms David wrote, "The law of the LORD is perfect, restoring the soul; the testimony of the LORD is sure, making wise the simple" (Ps. 19:7). David could have rebelled against God's laws. Even though he was the anointed king of Israel, he waited for years before he assumed Israel's throne.

Have you caught yourself wondering, *What is God up to in my life? Why are there so many heartaches and difficulties? Couldn't God step in and change my circumstances?* God can change anything that affects our lives. However, often a change of circumstances is not what we need. What we need is real wisdom to face the heartache and difficulties of our world. We also need to make a commitment to stay the course when life becomes difficult. This requires godly wisdom. Far too many people give up when the going gets rough. They seek an easier and faster way through life's challenges. But God wants us to learn how to seek Him and rely on His wisdom when trouble comes.

Is wisdom needed only in times of difficulty? No. If we fail to gain God's wisdom for our lives, then even in times of blessing, we will drift spiritually in our devotion to Him. We should strive toward the goal of remaining committed to God, no matter the circumstances.

I have talked with people who are struggling in the aftermath of poor decisions. Many, with pleading eyes, have asked, "What can I do to change all of this?" "How do I begin again after I have fallen to temptation?" "Is there any hope for my life?" The answer is yes! There is hope, and there is a way to start life over. We begin again in our devotion to God through prayer. This is where we can be the most vulnerable and open to God's presence. Prayer also provides the right opportunity for us to gain God's wisdom for every situation. If we will come to Him, He will direct our paths. There will be times when we make mistakes. Yet we can gain tremendous wisdom through our errors, especially when we ask God to show us where we have taken a wrong turn.

As we study the life of David, we quickly find that it is outlined with a deep love and affection for God. David also had a strong prayer life. He meditated on God's love and did not hesitate to seek the Lord's wisdom. While it seems that David spent much of his younger years running from a jealous king who sought to kill him, we know that God used this time of intense adversity to prepare him to rule over the nation of Israel. Patience and faith became synonymous with his life.

At times, we may wonder, *Lord, why am I having to face such heartache or trial?* Remember, God is near to us. He provides the wisdom we need even when grief and fear constrict our hearts. If we turn to Him in faith and cry out to Him, He will give us the ability to make wise decisions.

Is God still speaking to us today? Without a doubt. He speaks to those who know Him in one of three ways: through the reading of His Word, through a pastor or trusted Christian friend, or through the presence of the Holy Spirit who lives inside each believer. Faith is the one element that is crucial to gaining the wisdom of God. If you are faced with a difficult choice or challenge, God will provide the wisdom you need to make the correct decision. James wrote, "If any of you lacks wisdom, let him ask of God, who gives to all generously and without reproach, and it will be given to him. But he must ask in faith without any doubting, for the one who doubts is like the surf of the sea, driven and tossed by the wind" (James 1:5–6).

At one point, David could have taken Saul's life. David faced a serious decision, but because he had taken the necessary time to know God and meditate on His Word, he knew the right choice to make. He refused to harm Saul, who was God's anointed. Even though Saul deserved the opposite, David allowed him to live, and God blessed David's life abundantly because he had not acted with selfish motives.

God later said of David that he was a man after His own heart. David's life was not free of mistakes. Whenever he failed to exercise wisdom, he suffered grievous consequences. However, the overall view of David's life was one of wisdom and desire to please God.

The writer of Proverbs reminded us that "wisdom is supreme; therefore get wisdom. Though it cost all you have, get understanding" (Prov. 4:7 niv).

How do we gain the wisdom of God for our lives?

We gain wisdom when we seek God. If David came to a point where he did not know what to do, he would "inquire of the Lord." This is where our faith enters. We must believe, as James instructed us, that if we go to God with even the smallest detail, He will hear our prayer and answer it. This is exactly what He does. He will answer us in one of three ways: yes, no, or wait. If we sense His silence, then we should wait until He moves us forward.

We gain wisdom when we learn to meditate on God's Word. If we really want to receive a blessing, we must take our requests to God through prayer and then seek His guidance through His Word. God never will contradict His Word. Scripture provides a solution for every problem or decision we face. Scripture is not out of date. Therefore, we can trust the Word of God to provide the guidance we need.

We gain wisdom when we learn to obey the principles of Scripture.

Before David could rule as king, he had to learn to obey God. He also had to learn to follow the pathway God placed before him. This meant that he submitted his human desires to God. Some of David's desires were in keeping with God's plan for his life. However, David's desire to submit all that he was to God spoke volumes of his love for the Lord.

Do you love the Lord so much that you are willing to do what David did and release all that you have so God can live His life through you?

We gain wisdom as a result of prayer. In times of prayer, we learn to humble our hearts before God. We also learn to be quiet and listen for God's voice through the Holy Spirit who lives within each believer. God's word to us may come to our minds in the form of a Scripture. When it does, our spirits hear God's Word and immediately respond with gladness and thanksgiving.

We gain wisdom by observing how God works in our world. At times, the workings of the world may seem out of control. However, God is sovereign. He always is in control. Though our lives may be touched by death, sin, and sorrow, God is Lord over all, and He will bring purpose out of each event. He even uses the technology of this age to further His work of salvation on the earth.

We gain wisdom through wise counsel. Talk over your problems with trusted Christian friends, a counselor, or a pastor. Once they have given you their view or counsel, take this to God in prayer. If what they have told you is from God, it will not violate Scripture or any principle of God's Word.

We gain wisdom when we associate with wise people. Most people know when they have heard true wisdom. However, we must ask God to help us avoid deception. There are people who may seek to speak a "word of knowledge" to us. What they have to say may or may not be on target with God's plan for our lives.

You can avoid disappointment and feelings of discouragement when you ask God to sift what they have said to you through His infinite grid of wisdom. Never be afraid to say, "Thank you for praying for me, and I know you will understand when I tell you that I plan to seek God on this issue." Then go to God's Word for verification.

We seek wisdom to please God and to gain His perspective on our lives and individual situations. Here are the requirements for wisdom:

Have a strong determination to walk wisely. Our motivation for wisdom must begin and end with a love for God. We want to please Him. Therefore, we seek Him, and when we learn wisdom's way, we find that we are being conformed to the likeness of His Son.

Meditate on God's Word. God instructed Joshua to meditate on His Word day and night. The psalmist told us to hide the Word of God in our hearts (Ps. 119:11). Corrie ten Boom learned the value of this instruction during World War II. She was able to smuggle a few pages of God's Word into her Nazi prison cell. Later, she wrote, "Never before had I prayed as now. And I spoke to one who understood, who knew me and loved me. On Him I cast all my burdens."

Learn to be sensitive to the prompting of the Holy Spirit. The amazing part of seeking the wisdom of God is that we can learn to hear His voice. When the prophet Elijah lost his perspective, God spoke to him. However, the Lord's voice did not come to His prophet through an earthquake or storm. It came in the form of a still, quiet voice. When we are still—in our thoughts and emotions—God will speak to our hearts the way He did to Elijah. He commands us to "be still, and know that I am God" (Ps. 46:10 NKJV).

Believe God is the Source of wisdom. Faith and trust are necessary in gaining the wisdom of God. Human reasoning will fail you. Only the wisdom of God will guide you safely through life.

Have courage to obey God. Obedience reveals our true desire for wisdom. If we seek to obey God, then we are on the road to true wisdom. If we disobey the Lord, we must deal with our actions by seeking His forgiveness. There will be times when God will require us to go forward without knowing all that is ahead. The only way to do this is through having faith and through knowing that He is leading us. Blessings come to those who obey God. Therefore, we should be courageous and go forward by faith, trusting God to make our pathways safe.

Persevere. When you can say, "I know that I am doing the right thing. Therefore, I am going to keep my focus and continue on," then you are learning perseverance. The wisdom of God will come to you.

A STRONG AND MIGHTY FOUNDATION

You can lay a strong foundation for your life by asking God to come to you and, if you have never accepted His Son as your Savior, asking Him to come into your heart and forgive your sins. Realize the moment you do this, you are a child of God—a new creature in Christ—and you no longer stand at a distance from God. You belong to Him, and His eternal reward and blessing are yours to enjoy and experience from now until forever.

If you have drifted in your devotion to the Savior and feel as though each day you live you grow more distant in your relationship to God, then pray that He would draw you near to Himself. He knows your weaknesses, and if you will tell Him that you no longer want to be in charge of your life, He will come to you in a mighty way and bring hope and light to your dark and hopeless situation (Isa. 55:6–9).

SUGGESTED BIBLE READING

2 TIMOTHY 3:16; 4:3; 1 PETER 3:15; JOHN 14:6–17;
1 JOHN 5:14–15; MATTHEW 28:19–20; ROMANS
8:28; 12:1–2; 1 PETER 3:18; PSALMS 19:7; 32:8;
46:10; 66:18; 119:11; GALATIANS 5:22–23; EZEKIEL
28:12–15; 2 CORINTHIANS 4:4; 1 JOHN 4:4;
EPHESIANS 2:8–9; GENESIS 12:1; ACTS 16:6–7;
JAMES 1:4–6; 1 THESSALONIANS 5:17; PROVERBS
3:5–6; 4:7; COLOSSIANS 3:15; and ISAIAH 30:21;
55:6–9.

PRAYER

Dear heavenly Father, thank You for Your Word that is
a lamp to our feet and a light to our path. Please give
me a hunger to read it more faithfully and a mind to
understand it more clearly. Please show me how to
apply Your principles to my life. Amen.

JOURNAL QUESTIONS

- What is the Bible?

_____

_____

_____

- What is the Godhead?

_____

_____

_____

- What is salvation?

_____

_____

_____

- What is the Church?

_____

_____

_____

- What steps can you take to gain wisdom in life?

_____

_____

_____

The Bible is more than a series of rules and regulations; it is the living
Word of God. Discover how to handle the Bible and the reasons for
trusting it by visiting *www.InTouch.org*.

CONCLUSION

LIVING A LEGACY

When your life here on earth is over, how do you want to be remembered? What do you want people to say about you? What difference will it have made that you ever lived? What will you leave behind that has any lasting value?

The Bible says a great deal about death. The apostle Paul wrote, "For the wages of sin is death, but the free gift of God is eternal life in Christ Jesus our Lord" (ROM. 6:23). When Martha lamented the death of her brother, Lazarus, Jesus said, "Your brother will rise again . . . I am the resurrection and the life: he who believes in Me will live even if he dies, and everyone who lives and believes in Me will never die" (JOHN 11:23–25). Then in 1 CORINTHIANS 15, Paul dedicated forty-six verses to the subject of life after death, the promise of our resurrection. All through Scripture, we see that for those who believe in Christ, death is not the end of life. Our physical existence here on earth ends, but life continues with Christ in heaven.

There is nothing in the Bible about reincarnation; nor is there anything in the Scriptures about annihilation. We do not return to the earth as more enlightened beings or cease to exist after we die; we dwell either in heaven with God or in hell with Satan. But the life that we leave behind on earth is not entirely extinguished either. All of us—whether we want to or not—leave behind a legacy.

I've already covered the subjects of surrender to Christ and eternal security, and I hope that if you have not received Jesus Christ as your personal Savior, you will seriously consider doing so. If you have made that decision, my prayer is that you will grow closer to Him and more like Him every day. In closing this book, I want to talk about what we leave here on earth when we depart.

What kind of legacy will you leave behind when you die? What will be the message of your life? Think about this for a moment: you are alive because God gave you the gift of life. He gave you a body, a soul, and a spirit. He has equipped you with the abilities and talents that you need in order to accomplish His purpose for your life. He has a very specific will for you.

The problem is that many people do not even begin to ask, "What is God's personal will for my life?" Scripture tells us clearly that God has a twofold purpose in mind for His children: first, that we would be involved in good works, and second, that we would bring Him honor and glory. Paul said, "For by grace you have been saved through faith; and that not of yourselves, it is the gift of God; not as a result of works, so that no one may boast. For we are His workmanship, created in Christ Jesus for good works, which God prepared beforehand so that we would walk in them" (EPH. 2:8–10).

One of God's purposes for us is that our lives be characterized by good works. Paul said to Timothy, "Instruct them to do good, to be rich in good works, to be generous and ready to share, storing up for themselves the treasure of a good foundation for the future, so that they may take hold of that which is life indeed" (1 TIM. 6:18–19). We carry out God's intentions by investing our lives in those things that bring honor and glory to Him.

Jesus said, "Let your light shine before men in such a way that they may see your good works, and glorify your Father who is in heaven" (MATT. 5:16).

Unfortunately people are often more concerned about how long they will live than *how* they live. They think that having a lasting legacy means living a long life. But Scripture teaches us that God is more interested in what we do with the lives He has given us. When I think about longevity versus effectiveness, a man named Oswald Chambers comes to mind. You have probably heard of him; he wrote *My Utmost for His Highest*, the best-selling devotional of all time. Oswald Chambers was a man whose life was devoted entirely to God. Some say he was one of the greatest Christian thinkers of our time. He was born on July 24, 1874, in Aberdeen, Scotland, where he became a Christian during his teen years under the ministry of Charles Spurgeon. His death, the result of a ruptured appendix in 1917, left a tremendous void in the churches and fellowships he served.

After his death, a fellow worker remarked: "It is a mighty thing to see even once in a lifetime a man the self-expression of whose being is the Redemption of Jesus Christ manifested in daily hourly living. He would have simply called himself 'A believer in Jesus.'"[1] Though he lived only forty-two years, Oswald Chambers's work lives on today even more powerfully than it did while he was alive. His writings offer refuge and strength to many downcast souls—through his words, God continues to change lives for Christ's sake.

I first read Oswald Chambers's devotional as a college student. What impressed me most then—and still rings in my heart today—is that the most important thing, by far, is our personal relationship with Jesus Christ. Every time I pick up his devotional, I am blessed. He died nearly one hundred years ago, yet he is still alive today.

LIFE AFTER DEATH

When people consider life after death, they think mostly about what is going to happen to them when they get to heaven. Those who do not believe in Christ contemplate what will become of them if they don't go to heaven. But I want to focus on the part of our lives that remains here after we have gone.

I have known people who, despite living very short lives, left behind powerful, penetrating, and life-changing influences on others. You and I know that Jesus Christ lives today through those who have received Him as their personal Savior. A believer is simply a person through whom Jesus Christ is still living His life. Our lives are an expression of who He is.

You may think, *God couldn't use me that way.* Oh, yes, He can. Far too frequently, we minimize who we are and the potential that God has created in us. I am convinced we do this because we don't want the responsibility of living a godly life. We don't want to give account for our actions, so we hide behind a lack of talent or skill. But God has a purpose and a plan for each of His children, and He intends for us to fulfill it. He intends for us to leave a legacy that will affect others long after we are gone.

God has made eternal investments in each of our lives. First He gave us the awesome gift of life itself. Then He gave us redemption through His Son, Jesus Christ, so that we might live abundantly. He made it possible for us to understand our sinful condition, and through the amazing gift of faith, He made it possible for us to accept His forgiveness and to be indwelt by the Holy Spirit so, with His power, we could perform good works and bring glory to His name.

If you talk to your financial planner, he will tell you that your legacy is the material wealth, possessions, or property that you leave to those who survive you. But if such things are all we leave behind when we die, then those who don't have any money leave nothing, whereas the wealthy leave the best legacy, right? Wrong. Your real legacy is your life, your influence, and your testimony. This is what your loved ones will cherish most, and it is also what matters most to God.

You may think that compared to Oswald Chambers, you don't have much of a testimony. Wrong again. Everyone has a testimony—good or bad, strong or weak, rich or poor. You are building a legacy right now, in every day of your life. When you die, you will leave a witness for either good or evil.

What are you leaving? What do you want people to remember about you when you are gone? As an illustration, consider what various people in the Bible left. When I think about Abraham, I recall his great faith. That is still the message of Abraham's life. When I think about Moses, I remember the Ten Commandments that God gave him. When I think about David, the Psalms come to mind—they continue to bless me year after year. David has been gone for centuries, but his words of comfort and encouragement endure. Then I think about Solomon, and my mind goes immediately to the Proverbs, an awesome collection of divinely inspired literature that offers eternal wisdom to those who read it. What about the apostle Paul? He was beset by terrible obstacles and suffered immensely, but he left us letters and epistles that give hope, guidance, and encouragement to millions. I read Paul's works nearly every day of my life; as I read Ephesians, Colossians, Philippians, and his letters to Timothy, I am continuously blessed. And look at the legacy of the Lord Jesus Christ. In the short thirty-three years He lived on the earth, He altered history forever. Through Him, we can live extraordinary lives despite our fallen condition.

Think about people who have left an indelible mark on history. The men who founded America—who established our republic and gave us the Constitution—left an awesome legacy for millions who live in freedom as a result. Think about the hymn writers, who gave us words of worship. Fanny Crosby, one of the most prolific hymn writers of all time, was blinded by a doctor who misdiagnosed her illness. Now, more than a century after her death, people are still singing, "Blessed assurance, Jesus is mine! O what a foretaste of glory divine!" That is her legacy.

The list goes on. Even in our generation, great people are living out their legacies. I think about Dr. Bill Bright who left us Campus Crusade, the greatest missionary discipleship movement in history. This momentous ministry is discipling believers all over the world. Dr. Bright was a quiet, unassuming man, but he followed Christ's command: "Go into all the world and preach the gospel to all creation." He gave his life to the Great Commission, and his obedience changed many lives.

I've mentioned the great people about whom most of us have heard, but what about the "ordinary" people? There is a woman seldom acknowledged, but she is a perfect example of what I'm talking about. When Paul was writing his second epistle to encourage Timothy during a trial, he said to the young minister: "I am mindful of the sincere faith within you, which first dwelt in your grandmother Lois and your mother Eunice, and I am sure that it is in you as well" (2 TIM. 1:5). Lois's profound faith was carried down through Eunice to Timothy. Her faith became a living part of Timothy's ministry.

The impact of parents and grandparents on children's lives is truly incredible. Very few people have ever heard of George Washington Stanley, but my grandfather left me a few simple truths that live on in my life today. One of those truths is this: obey God and leave all the consequences to Him. I remember vividly the day I sat on his front porch and asked him how to succeed in life. He described obedience this way: "If God tells you to put your head through a wall, you get up and start running. And when you get to the wall, He'll provide a hole in it." My grandfather's sage wisdom concerning obedience is the basis upon which I make my decisions today. He left me a legacy for which I shall ever be grateful. Far more important than any financial inheritance is the wisdom that he left me, which has enveloped and guided my life.

And then there is the legacy my mother left me. She did not have an easy life. I watched her endure constant hardships and trials. I witnessed her persistence and perseverance. She always said to me, "Never give up. Do your best; be your best; look your best. Be what God wants you to be." Her perspective and tenacity are instilled within my heart and mind. She left me something that is far more valuable than anything money can buy; she left me an example. I learned far more from my mother by watching her live than by listening to what she said.

You have a legacy, and you are living it right now. The question is, what do you want to leave? I'm not a great politician or a hymn writer, but God has given me a very specific purpose in life. He's given you a purpose too. He's given all of us good works to do for the kingdom of God. What are you living for? Is it to perform good works because you love God and you want your life to have eternal value? It's time to take this question seriously and make your life count. One of the most horrible things I can think of is coming to the end of life and looking back with regret, thinking, *What difference have I made?*

What difference does your life make? What are your goals? God created you for the purpose He wants to accomplish through your life. Consider the following questions:

Will you leave your children a love for the Word of God? If you have children or grandchildren, then more than likely, you have thought about what you are going to leave them. Will they be able to look back and say, "I saw my mom and my dad reading the Scriptures. I heard them reading the Word of God. I heard my parents talking about how God spoke to them through a verse. I watched as they responded to God's Word. I heard them talking about decisions they made based on guidance from Scripture"? Will they love and trust the Word of God? When they go to school and hear a professor criticize the Bible, will they be able to stand strong and defend the infallible, inerrant Word of the living God? If you do not hand down to them a stalwart faith in God's Word, you leave them vulnerable to the empty philosophies of our age.

Will your children inherit the legacy of praying parents? How many times has your son or your daughter ever seen you on your knees crying out to God during difficulty and hardship? Are you going to leave your children the inescapable picture of you on your knees talking to your heavenly Father?

I remember when I realized how important this image was to children. I was pastoring my first church in North Carolina. My son, Andy, was about two years of age, but he could communicate well. I remember lying on a particular rug where I would pray; I was stretched out on the floor talking to God. I turned and opened my eyes and saw little Andy stretched out beside me looking me right in the eye, saying, "What are you doing?" It was a cute incident, but I think about how many times he and I stretched out together in the following years to talk to God. He never forgot it, and I never forgot either.

Your visible and audible prayer life becomes an indelible picture that God imprints on your children's minds. That's how important prayer is. Have you ever said to your children, "We really need to pray and ask God to give us direction about this"? Can they remember you talking about how God answered your prayers? The wonderful thing about families eating together is that mealtime becomes an opportunity to discuss how God answered your prayers that day. Let your children talk about how He answered their prayers at school and how He's meeting their needs. Thank God for caring enough to listen and be personally involved in your lives.

Will your children remember you taking them to church? Will they remember that you made it your habit week after week to worship the living God? That you weren't going to church because you felt compelled or obligated, but because of your deep love for the Lord Jesus Christ? Do they hear you singing hymns as you stand beside them? Do they see you open your Bible as the pastor opens his? Do they see you taking notes during the sermon because what you are hearing is important enough to remember? Will they recall you asking them, "Remember what the pastor said today?"

How have your children learned to spend their time and money? Another gift we can leave our children is the example of how to use the resources of time and money. How much time in any given week do you give to the Lord's work in order to bring Him glory and honor? Your time is not your own; it belongs to God. The very gift of life itself is time: seconds, minutes, weeks, and years. God has given us this precious resource, and He is going to call us home to give an account for it. I'm not saying that everyone must go into professional ministry as a career, but serving God should be your first priority.

What about your finances? Do you spend at least a portion of your money investing in things that will last for eternity? Will your children remember you giving the first 10 percent of your earnings back to God even when it didn't seem that you could afford to? One of the best ways to teach your children trust is by giving to God's work and allowing them to witness firsthand how He multiplies your investment. When they see you giving to God and waiting to see what He does with your tithe, they inherit a conviction about His provision for their lives.

On the other hand, many parents do not realize what a terrible legacy they leave when they don't give to the Lord's work. They are sending a loud and clear message: we can't trust God to provide for our physical needs. Our children will pay closer attention to our actions than the platitudes we offer. We might tell them that it is important to make the Lord our highest priority, but if they never see us pray, read the Bible, spend time with Him, or give to His work, they will have no reason to follow our advice.

What are you leaving your children? If it's only money, forget it! That simply will not last for eternity. What you plant in your children's hearts—the spiritual truths you sow in their lives—is the real legacy you leave.

THE LEGACY OF YOUR WITNESS

One of the most important aspects of your legacy is your Christian witness. If you take the Great Commission seriously and share the gospel with others and invest in missionary work, that legacy will be multiplied in countless people long after you are gone. Do your children hear you talk about sharing the gospel? Imagine that a boy or girl mustered up enough courage to witness to someone at school and then came home excited about the opportunity, but Dad changed the subject. This is a disaster—in doing this, the parent blunts the very spirit of the child who is trying to do what God desires. Mothers and fathers, your children need your support—and example—for godly behavior. Encouraging them spiritually is a significant part of your legacy.

The scenario I just mentioned is all too common. I know many young people who desire to follow God, but must do so against the wishes of their parents. Many young people go to college and prepare for a career as an engineer, lawyer, or doctor. Then God calls them to preach or become a missionary, and they have the terrible task of going home and telling their parents. Far too many receive guilt and condemnations from their parents for choosing the path that offers less commercial stability. When God gets hold of your children, you ought to be motivated and inspired! Your reaction and attitude about their spiritual pursuits form an important part of the legacy you leave.

Likewise, the way you react to difficulty in times of persecution, suffering, and pain is a part of what you leave the next generation. Your children will remember your pattern of response in tough times. Do you refuse to give up and walk away? Do you reject the chance to take a pill or a drink? Do you refrain from complaining? When they see you put your trust in the living God, they will do the same.

Keep in mind that your children aren't the only beneficiaries of your legacy. How many of your friends have heard about Jesus? How many of your coworkers have heard you talk about Christ? How many neighbors hear you express what you believe about God's Word and how He has answered your prayers in the most awesome ways? Are you ashamed of the gospel?

Oftentimes a person who is sitting nearby is hoping that someone will speak a work of encouragement. How many opportunities do you miss? Whether you know it or not, you are leaving a legacy. It will be strong, penetrating, motivating, and life changing, or it will be weak and wasted.

Now, imagine that you are eighty-five years old, looking back over your life. God has answered your prayers, met your needs, and worked in your life, but you never shared your stories with anybody. There is no record of what He did—you never wrote it down. The only testimony you have of all the wonderful things God did for you is a few fading memories.

I once said to my son, Andy, "I've hidden away my diaries because I don't want anybody to read them right now." He said, "Dad, don't worry about it. Your handwriting is so bad, they couldn't read them even if they saw them!" That amusing comment made me start journaling on a computer.

Think about it—if you never record God's involvement in your life, you are depriving your children and grandchildren of a priceless treasure. Imagine them picking up a book full of true stories about how God provided for you, the principles He taught you, and the prayers He answered. You can't afford to soak up blessing after blessing and just ignore the beneficiaries of God's grace in your life.

My grandfather left me a legacy of wonderful, godly principles and examples, but I'd give a great deal to have a day-by-day or even week-by-week account of his relationship with Jesus Christ and how God worked in his life.

At a recent book signing, I met a young lady who made quite an impression on me. She knelt down by the table and told me that her father had passed away two months earlier, and she went to his home on the West Coast to handle his affairs. In going through his things, she found a big box full of audio and videotapes. Her curiosity got the best of her, and she decided to listen to one of them. Then she listened to another and another. When she left, she packed up a bunch of them and took them back home with her to distribute among friends. It turns out she didn't know her father very well while he was living, but through listening to the sermons he collected, she found what he treasured in life. She knelt there beside me weeping in thanksgiving that she finally knew what her dad was really like.

You are leaving a legacy—whether you want to or not. The question is, what will it be? Long after we die, the example of who we are lives on. Will your example be for good or for evil? Saddam Hussein boasted that Joseph Stalin was his mentor. That should be no surprise to anyone—both are two of the most wicked people who ever lived. The legacy of Joseph Stalin was the murder of millions, and his "beneficiary" emulated him well. That is an extreme example, but it illustrates an important truth. People observe you when you don't even know they are watching, and what they learn from you is your legacy to them.

Let your legacy be a reflection of generosity, selflessness, compassion, and love. Consider the ways that God is working in your life today. How will He continue to work through your example and gifts when you are no longer here? I encourage you to be intentional, not just about your impact here and now, but with regard to your influence for Jesus Christ throughout eternity.

SUGGESTED BIBLE READING

ROMANS 6:23; JOHN 11:23–25; 1 CORINTHIANS 15;
EPHESIANS 2:8–10; 1 TIMOTHY 6:18–19;
2 TIMOTHY 1:5.

PRAYER

Dear heavenly Father, I thank You for the priceless,
life-changing legacy Jesus Christ left for me to inherit.
I pray that You will enable me to leave His legacy to
my children and loved ones and to share it with people
I know here on earth. In Christ's name I pray. Amen.

JOURNAL QUESTIONS

- What is the Great Commission?

_____

_____

_____

_____

_____

- What legacy did your parents and grandparents leave you?

_____

_____

_____

_____

- What is your legacy?

_____

_____

_____

_____

God has called His church to the task of making disciples.
Learn how He's accomplishing this mission
at _www.InTouch.org._

AFTERWORD

In MATTHEW 6:33 Jesus said, "Seek first His kingdom and His righteousness, and all these things will be added to you." There is an incredible promise in this Scripture: "*All* these things will be added to you." Jesus meant what He said, or He was not telling the truth. We know that God cannot lie. Therefore, His promise is real. And it is available to all who love Him enough to live by His ways.

We can think of the kingdom in terms of the principles of our Creator. If we live by the principles God has established, He will assume full responsibility for our lives and give us everything we need to live an extraordinary life. The problem is that people often convince themselves that there is some great mystery to discovering the secret of fulfillment in life. Easily distracted by their own vanity, they chase after material things and worldly success and are never happy. Because they don't want to live according to God's Word—thinking that doing so will somehow restrict their lifestyle—they shut out the very source of true happiness.

In her book *Tramp for the Lord*, Corrie ten Boom tells of the time she visited a hospital where polio patients were being treated. The doctor in charge asked her if she would like to speak to the patients, but the sight of their suffering was too much for her. "No," she replied, "I think I am unable to talk. I just want to go off somewhere and cry."

But a moment later, she changed her mind. As she stood beside the bed of a man who could barely breathe, she told him about Jesus Christ, who suffered for each of us. Corrie writes,

> I finished speaking and from my bag took a small embroidery. On one side was stitched a beautiful crown. The other side was quite mixed up. "When I see you on this bed," I said, "not speaking, not moving, I think of this embroidery. Your life is like this. See how dark it is. See how the threads are knotted and tangled, mixed up. But when you turn it around then you can see that God is actually weaving a crown for your life. God has a plan for your life and He is working it out in beauty." He picked up a pencil and wrote: *Thank God I am already seeing the beautiful side.* What a miracle!

Many people today are like that patient. They may not lie in a hospital bed, but their hearts are sick with discouragement, fear, and doubt. God has prepared for them an extraordinary life that they cannot seem to grasp. Thankfully our God is merciful and faithful, and the way to that wonderful life is simple. Living by God's principles is the clear path to the extraordinary life. God does not lie to or mislead His followers. His offer for abundant life is a true promise for us and for generations to come. If you have not received Christ as your personal Savior, I challenge you to compare your life with the one He offers. If you make Him Lord of your life, He will change you in ways so extraordinary, your passion and love for Him will outlive you.

NOTES

PRINCIPLE 1

1. Raymond V. Edman, *They Found the Secret* (Grand Rapids, MI: Zondervan, 1984), 18.
2. Ibid., 19–20.

PRINCIPLE 4

1. Oswald Chambers, *My Utmost for His Highest,* July 5 Devotion, edited by James Reimann (Grand Rapids, MI: Discovery House Press, 1992).

PRINCIPLE 9

1. George Barna, *Growing True Disciples,* (Colorado Springs, CO: Waterbrook Press, 2001), 65.

CONCLUSION

1. David McCagland, *Abandoned to God: The Life Story of My Utmost for His Highest,* (Oswald Chambers, Pub., 1993).

ABOUT THE AUTHOR

Through his 50 years of ministry, Dr. Charles F. Stanley has become known as "America's Pastor" for his dedication to leading people worldwide into a growing relationship with Jesus Christ. Dr. Stanley is the founder and president of In Touch Ministries, whose *In Touch* radio and television program can be heard around the world in more than 100 languages. He has also been Senior Pastor of First Baptist Church in Atlanta, Georgia since 1971.

Dr. Stanley received his bachelor of arts degree from the University of Richmond, his bachelor of divinity degree from Southwestern Baptist Theological Seminary, and his master's degree and doctorate from Luther Rice Seminary. He has twice been elected president of the Southern Baptist Convention and is a *New York Times* best-selling author, having written more than 50 books, including *Living the Extraordinary Life, When the Enemy Strikes, Finding Peace, God Is In Control, Pathways to His Presence, Success God's Way, Charles Stanley's Handbook for Christian Living, The Source of My Strength, How to Listen to God, Life Principles Bible,* and his latest release, *Landmines in the Path of the Believer.*

OTHER BOOKS BY CHARLES STANLEY

THE LIFE PRINCIPLES SERIES

God wants you to live an extraordinary life, and He has gone out of His way to make it possible. He has provided His Son as your Savior, His Holy Spirit as your Counselor and Teacher, and His Word as your infallible guide. We want to help you on your spiritual journey. The purpose of the Charles Stanley Institute for Christian Living is to provide Christians worldwide with biblical truths on which to build a solid, practical foundation for abundant living. Take the next step in your walk of faith today at www.InTouch.org

Go to www.InTouch.org
for a FREE
subscription or call
Customer Care at
1-800-789-1473

In Touch Ministries

SEARCH [   ] GO

HOME   ABOUT US   BROADCASTS   MAGAZINE   LIFE PRINCIPLES   GLOBAL OUTREACH   GET INVOLVED   BOOKSTORE   CONTACT US

Welcome to In Touch Ministries Online!

Welcome to In Touch Ministries Online!

We reach the world with the good news of Jesus Christ through the teaching of Dr. Charles Stanley. Our television and radio broadcasts, podcasts, and magazine introduce people to the life-changing gospel.

✟ New Believer's Kit   📄 Life Principles Notes   🛒 Buy this week's message.

WATCH   LISTEN   DONATE

Early Light Devotional

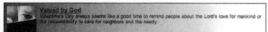

Valued by God
Valentine's Day always seems like a good time to remind people about the Lord's love for mankind or our responsibility to care for neighbors and the needy.

What's New

In the Life Principles Center
This week Dr. Charles Stanley discusses Life Principle 9: Trusting God means looking beyond what we can see to what God sees. Watch the video.

The In Touch Impact Prayer Team
The Impact Prayer Team prays for lives to be changed forever. To learn more about how to become a part of the team, click here.

Feature Articles

Where Are You, Lord?
When the Lord is silent, you have only one reasonable option—trust Him.
Dr. Stanley explains how to wait in confidence. Read more.

When God Is Silent
Bible Study: How should a Christian respond when God seems quiet in the midst of adversity? Find out in this study. Read more.

Protecting Your Thoughts
Did you know a single thought can be the first step into habitual sin? How can you protect your mind? Read more.

LIFE LESSON
OF THE DAY

God tells us to obey His commands—all of them—not merely the ones we like or understand (1 Sam. 1:15).

Visit the Life Principles Center

FEATURED RESOURCE

The Life Principles Bible
This Bible combines Scripture with the principles that guide Dr. Stanley's life and empower his ministry. Order your copy.

Visit the In Touch Bookstore

Our mission is to lead people worlwide into a growing relationship with Jesus Christ and to strengthen the local church.

AVAILABLE NOW

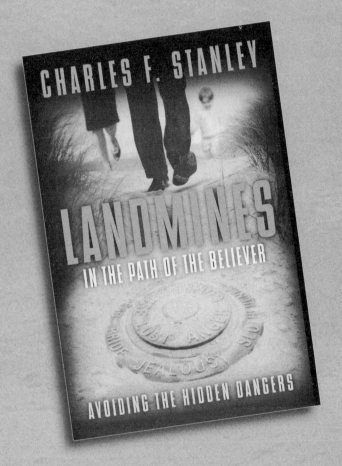

AVAILABLE
NOW

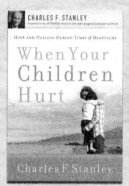
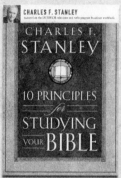
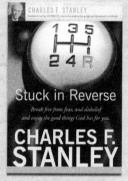

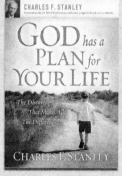
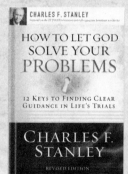

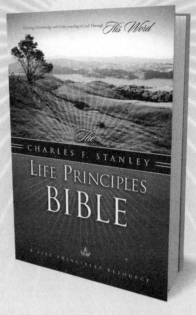

The CHARLES F. STANLEY LIFE PRINCIPLES BIBLE delivers Stanley's cherished values to benefit every Christian in their life's pursuits. With almost 200,000 in print, The *Charles F. Stanley Life Principles Bible* communicates the life principles Dr. Stanley has gleaned from the Word through his years of Bible teaching and pastoral ministry. The result is a Bible overflowing with practical articles, notes, and sidebars that help readers understand what the Bible has to say about life's most important questions.

Features include:

- 30 Life Principles, with articles throughout the Bible
- Life Lessons
- Life Examples from the people of the Bible
- "Answers to Life's Questions" articles
- God's Promises for Life index to get into the Scripture Book Introductions
- "What the Bible Says About" articles
- Concordance
- Available in both the New King James Version and New American Standard Bible

JOURNAL NOTES

JOURNAL NOTES

JOURNAL NOTES

JOURNAL NOTES

JOURNAL NOTES

JOURNAL NOTES

JOURNAL NOTES

JOURNAL NOTES